WHERE'S MY PENSION?

Truth
As Strange
As Fiction:

A Tale of
Jacob Bowles

By John Pierce

Introduction

I was at a standstill. At first, this had seemed such a simple quest. The records and memories of these people must be somewhere, but where?

No, I don't work for the Missing Persons Bureau. Nor am I in the hire of the FBI, the CIA, or any other secret organization. I am not in the research department of a Private Investigator, and I am not working on a case for a newspaper, or some high-profile attorney. So why am I so driven to pinpoint the vital statistics, the relationships, and the homes of these people?

All right, I admit it. I was doing my own form of private investigation – genealogical research. But to me, it was the same as working for the Missing Persons Bureau or doing research for a high-profile attorney. Have you ever enjoyed figuring something out, putting all the pieces together? Conquering an intricate jigsaw puzzle? Poring through a well-designed mystery novel, in which the clues are presented in such a way that you gradually come to the right conclusions, (with no red herrings or last-minute insights)? Playing a video game where you must discover items that fit together to point to the next clue? Becoming enraptured with the quest of some long lost artifact – the Holy Grail, the ancient tomb, the sunken treasure?

Well, I was caught up in the thrill of the hunt. The clues, though, were petering out. Doors which had so far failed to yield continued to resist with what seemed even more resistance. Doors which I had previously opened just sat there, hanging open, with nothing new on the other side.

And then, seemingly from nowhere, I discovered an unrelated story of human tragedy, treachery, frustration, deception, abandonment, false, failed (or even contrived) memories, intrigue, investigations, sworn testimonies, and at the end, a heap of unanswered questions. I hope that you have a basic interest in problem-solving, and that this will be of interest to you.

MY GENEALOGICAL BACKGROUND –THE THRILL OF THE HUNT

This is a thumbnail of what one might encounter while doing genealogical research. I realize there are many different methods today, and pervasive information on the internet. This is a small glimpse into what I encountered prior to the explosion of electronic information. This is the plodding side of research.

My excitement level was rising. Spurred on by a series of successes on my mother's side of the family, both from research that other family members had done, as well as a very distinctive surname, I was sure that with a few well-placed discoveries the same could be done on my father's side.

Imagine my frustration, then, when I discovered that my grandmother on my father's side apparently decided one day that whatever memorabilia was stored in her house was just taking up too much space, and was worthless anyway, so she threw it all out. To her, the dead past was exactly that: dead, and past. There was no point in using up space reserved for the present and for the future with what might as well be dust. To further frustrate matters, in trying to contact other living members of her family's line, I've encountered very little interest in that branch of our history. There is a sense that somewhere in the past there was a family "split," and maybe even a name change (although, so far I have found no evidence of either). And where there may have been some "reluctance to associate" due to one family member's seeming to chase after young skirts, the records I have found do not support that position. But in this line of endeavor, finding no evidence is proof of nothing. One might as well have not engaged in the search in the first place.

Brushing off my initial discouragement, I determined to take whatever little information I had and plow through the tedious work of searching public records for the family ties I sought. My thoughts at this time were fuzzy – based on initial success I was overly optimistic, but as new doors became harder and harder to find I was losing hope.

I began with straightforward assumptions. We all have two biological grandmothers and two biological grandfathers. That's just a fact of life, unless and until today's scientific gods formulate ways to circumvent that detail of human reproduction. For some of us, that in itself is not enough to define our family history. Our grandfathers may have been divorced or widowed, remarried or simply lived with someone else who raised the children. Some of us may have grown up knowing one or both of our grandparents, others may have little recollection, depending on family ties, geographical distances, or our age when our grandparents died.

For some, that is enough to satisfy us today about our heritage: I am here today, the offspring of a man and a woman, who were each offspring of a man and a woman. What is the point of knowing anything more about prior generations? Their lives are over – they had their opportunity – and now I am on the stage. Others have a desperate need to know everything there is to know (and some, everything there is to be speculated), whether for religious reasons, pride, or personal gain. They are determined to discover every single one of their ancestors, either to "own" them as a part of their extended family, or at least to find, perhaps, if only to find that one, valuable, elusive link to royalty and fame. And still others are simply consumed by the challenge of the quest – how well can I utilize all the historical information available to discover the secrets of my family's past? Almost like an archaeological dig, there are shards to be unearthed and pieced together, until the whole piece of ancient pottery (granted, it is probably cracked and marred) stands before us.

I find myself in the last category. I want to find what there is to know, accurately. Speculation may be worthwhile, but only if it opens possibilities that eventually result in confirmation. To what end? I guess I'm touching lives that once were lived here on earth, people who actually lived history, getting a glimpse of the heritage that we have received.

So how does one go about digging up information from the past? Let's look at what we, as individuals, can do. First, we can quiz our immediate family, parents, and hopefully uncles, aunts and grandparents. Is this information reliable? Hopefully it is, although as we will later see, memories can be either very fickle or very contrived. Then we extend it, maybe from "both ends." Having taken the family as far back as possible, can we then find corroborative evidence for the family beyond them? Can we find brothers and sisters, neighboring families, contemporary documents?

"Oh," I hear you protesting. "That sounds terribly tedious and boring!" Perhaps, for you, the thrill of discovery is about as exciting as stubbing your toe. Not so for me – the opportunity to open a new historical trail in my family is a natural high. And I had to start somewhere.

My first attempt, compared to what I can do today via the internet and commercial genealogy services was almost pathetic. I decided to trek to the nearest cache of national archives, where I knew I should be able to find indexes to various government records, as well as microfilm copies of all available census records. This would be a reasonably reliable source of information, since, by and large, there was no prior bias in the generation of the records. There may be other issues here –

people lying to census takers, neighbors giving information for missing families, record takers who cannot write, index-makers who cannot read – but, hopefully a preponderance of evidence that agrees over a number of years could give me some valid clues.

So, here I am, ready to attack this data supply, and what is in my arsenal? What is required in order to find the needles of my research in the haystacks of data that are archived here? Let's see, I've got a handful of surnames, and some rough guesses as to when the fathers of the families should be in the census entries. But what then? What if I don't know the name of the father I'm looking for? (And forget the mother – unless she was divorced or widowed she probably won't show up in any census index.) Hopefully, I'll have an idea of the area where the family lived. That should narrow down my search! So, I have the memories of my living relatives, back as far as they go, and then I just look for the next census back, close to the last known location of the family, for either the same family ten years earlier or else the father of unknown name who has a son of the correct name to connect the dots!

That should be enough for a first start. So with great anticipation (I am about to UNLOCK DOORS!) I drive to the local depository of national archives. This should be a fruitful expedition – after all, I have at least two to three hours to collect all the information I need. Today, I am going to harvest **tons** of new facts and clues. I am armed with locations (Kentucky and Pennsylvania), names (both paternal and maternal grandparents and great-grandparents), and the years to search – 1890, 1880, 1870, 1860, 1850, 1840, 1830 …

So in I go, past the security gate; "I'm doing genealogical research;" to the desk, collect a ticket assigning me one of the microfilm readers, and…

Now what? Let's see, they have this section down at the end with computers and a CD-ROM reader that has all sorts of different information – marriages, land records, immigration lists. They have rows upon rows of file cabinets, filled with the microfilm records of the various censuses. Oh, my, they have indexes here for soldiers in the various wars. Were any of my relatives in the Civil War, or the Revolutionary War? Probably, but who could they be? I'd better make a note to try to track that down. What was it that I came here for? For now, I'd best not let myself be distracted.

Onward to the census records. Which ones should I try first, the ones I'm virtually positive about, or the more difficult? I suppose it would be best to get used to the system first, and verify some of my current information. (Ouch, I've nearly spent half an hour here and I've barely learned where things are in the room!) I must just be careful and efficient. Select the correct year and state from the index books on the side wall. Here it is. Let's see, the names are in alphabetical order, so that's a plus. I'll turn to one of the surnames of my family, one that is very distinctive and therefore should be easy to find. And, voila! Hmmm, but these are spelled so many different ways. And they're in different locations: that means, different spools of microfilm.

I'm afraid there's no easy way around this. I'd best copy down all the information from the index – name, location, microfilm number, so that I can do my search without having to return to the index book. Then, locate the file with the desired microfilm cartridges, select a few of them, and take them to the booth that has my ticket number on it to scan the images and "find my people." (And now I've been here an hour and I'm still just starting my search.)

You can probably guess how this will go – it seems so true to all of life. The booths are dimly lit, since the goal here is to see some information from a miniature, dark film copy with just enough light shining through it to get a clear image. There is barely enough room at the front and sides of the reader to place the reels I've brought. I want to be able to take notes from the images I find, but there is only a little lip of table space left, and because it's so dim, it's hard to see what I'm writing. The microfilm reels snap onto one side of the reader, and, hopefully, there is a take-up reel at the reader that is the correct size for the film I want to read. There is a lever for positioning, a knob for focus, sometimes something to alter the angle or the amount of light in order to improve the image. Then there is the handle attached to the crank that winds the film from one reel to the other. Hopefully, the last person to use the reel rewound it after use. And then, after all that, I find that the image I am looking for is image 515 out of 517. So I begin cranking. And cranking.

But, finally, it all seems worth it. There, before me, is real honest-to-goodness information about real honest-to-goodness people living in a family in a real honest-to-goodness location where a census taker collected their names, ages, sex, and place-of-birth. This is what I came here for – a true glimpse of the past. Now I could, if I wanted, remove the reels from this unit and take them to the front to have them photo-copied for 25c, but there's too much I want to get done right now. So I grab my pen and paper and, as quickly as possible in these cramped quarters, copy down the information from the census form.

Later, the overwhelming scope of this task begins to dawn on me. There are so many entries – some that might be relatives of mine, living near known relations, but just unknown to me. So do I copy down whole pages of data, to go over later, or do I simply grab the information I know is pertinent now, and come back later to fill in the gaps? And sometimes the data is right there in front of me, but it's illegible scribbles, or too faded to be of much use.

Remember that seemingly huge chunk of time that I had available to track down my family's past? Like sand, it slipped through my fingers. At the end, I barely had time to grab a few more census indexes and search for pertinent surnames, take down the microfilm roll numbers for future reference, and then bid the archives farewell.

Modern technology has been a boon to all sorts of information research and data analysis. This is just as true in genealogical and historical research as in any other field. There are new and imaginative software packages, word processors, and the internet. Commercial genealogical sites have made available census and other related historical information that is more fully indexed than that found in the National Archives. Indeed, it is now possible to search most of the U.S. census records on any name included in the census – not just heads of households. This is an incredible boon, especially for the case where one year the head of a household is known, but 10 years earlier he was "somebody's" son, and we don't know the somebody. Before, our search would have needed to examine every possible somebody. But now, we can reduce the effort by searching on the name of the son.

Alas, even with these luxuries, we are hardly out of the woods. One year the entry might be found as D. J. Somebody, another year as Drew Sombod, maybe another year as James D. Sumbods. And the age may flit around, depending on who took the census and who was giving the information. If the person who transcribed the name couldn't quite make out the name, either because they weren't used to reading the old-style script, or because the original script is just unreadable, we might even need to look for something like O. Z. Linnaby.

COMBINING REASONED SPECULATION WITH INTUITIVE LEAPS

So what was the net result of my efforts in sifting through all the seemingly endless facts in that vast repository of data? Were all the dots connected? Had I now confidently found my ancestors, back through my great-great grandfathers, say? Hardly! In fact, by little wisps and tendrils I had barely extended the edges of my research, and in some instances introduced more questions than answers.

But, in retrospect, it was a commendable accomplishment. I had started with a list of names, great uncles and aunts mentioned to me by a brother of my father, and had begun to see evidence of their ancestors in the public records of this land. How so? In part, because of the nature and habit of the human race – we tend to name our children based on some prior connection, usually a previous family name, and often a previous family surname. Find enough of these connected, and the suspicions can grow into traceable leads. Of course, the numerous misspellings and illegible scrawlings obscure the trail, but that just makes the search harder, not necessarily impossible.

Interestingly, I found connections two generations back more quickly than those which were more current, simply because the records were easier to find, and not because of any great effort on my part. In fact, the more recent records were particularly difficult to track down – at times, I began to think that maybe some of my ancestors were determined to remain out of the public eye, finding a new place to hide every time the census taker came by. Their names just did not seem to show up in any of the census indexes.

Well, if they are not in the index, but you are convinced they must surely be somewhere, what are the options? At last, the most tedious option presents itself: perform a manual search of all the records. Of course, in that case you can hope that you have enough information to begin the search in the right place. Where is that to be? If you found them ten years earlier, or ten years later, are they in the same location? Or have they moved throughout the nation, in search of the American dream? If they have moved, your hopes of finding them will be quite dim – so you must start with the hope that they have not moved. Locate the proper township, and begin scanning the records for a familiar name....

Sometimes, in the midst of this tedious quest, the serendipitous occurs. While (somewhat fruitlessly) poring over the records for the township of Butler, in Butler County, Pennsylvania, I chanced upon this delightful entry by the census taker in 1880 (an entry which I believe captures a glimpse of the humanity and the history of another point in time). You can only imagine the difficulty of traveling through this location. The census taker voices his complaint –

"It is a Bout Four Square and Sirounds the Borow Off Butler and is Cut from North East to South West that is from one Corner, to the Other By a large Creek Caled Connoquessning Creek, Whitch passes through Butler Borrow, Township All around Borrow, Besides the Creek Thare is Several Other Streams of Water Little Connoquessing Passes across North West Corner of Said Township it is very Difficult to Travel this Township on Account of the Streames or Creeks. And the Borow of Butler in It, Allthough don't under me Its all Bourrow and Creeks."

No wonder some of the census entries are incomplete! Not only are these poor census takers poorly paid, but far too much is requested of them in the way of commitment.

For a researcher, where do reasoned speculation and intuitive leaps yield accurate and dependable results? If I find a head of household named George, in 1860, who is 23 years old, how can I be sure that George, age 15, with the same last name, living in some other household in 1850, is or is not the same George? Or what if his name is Harry, but the George in 1860 is George H.? And then, moving backwards in history, what happens in 1840 and before, where census records have only the head of household, and no family members?

This was becoming my dilemma. I had a number of candidates for family members, but there were either no direct connections from one census year to the next (what with the 10-year gaps), or else there just was not enough other corroborating evidence to have any level of assurance. Take the case of one person with the correct last name, living by himself in 1860, 21 years of age, a "shoemaker" in Pennsylvania. Was he perhaps a member of the same family as my great-great grandfather (of whom I could not even find any record in 1860)? In 1850, someone of the same name <u>was</u> in that family, but his age was 9. Is that close enough, or is this just a coincidental miss? In 1870, someone of the same name is now 29 and has a family (children 6, 4 and 2), with a wife from France. In 1880, a man of the same name has a family with three children of the same names, now 16, 14 and 12), but with a wife whose name and place of origin are different, and another child who didn't show up 10 years earlier. Ten years later is 1890, and just when it might have been nice to have a little more confirmation, we encounter a year when most census records were destroyed. So there is no help there, and by the time 1900 rolls around, the traces seem to have disappeared. Yet, in 1910, I find someone with the correct name and age (but still a different wife??), and then working back to

1900, find the same man and wife, although his age is all wrong. Can anything be done to reconcile all of this information?

Fortunately, there is one great event which helps to span the empty years between the census documents. This is the War of the Rebellion, America's great Civil War. At least, it becomes a source of valuable information if the family member who served was convinced they had been disabled during the war. In this particular case, a pension record existed that concurred with the information I found in the 1910 census: same name, same wife, same state. Perhaps, if sufficient detail could be found in the information held in the documents surrounding the pension application, I would be able to determine whether, in fact, this person was a member of my extended family.

Little did I imagine what I would actually unearth. Naïvely, I had assumed that the facts exposed by the various census records were simply variants of the same well-defined family, perhaps a wife's middle name one year instead of her first name, a little mistake in place of birth (New York or Canada, say, being just a border away from each other), a slight variation in the year of birth. I pictured families who stayed mainly in one location, and stayed mainly intact, with straight-line projections of their residences over ten years from one census to the next. And yet, although I did find the confirmation of the sought-for family bond, it was surrounded by a human drama that included war injuries, pleas for justice, sworn testimonies, unreliable memories or just flat-out lies, and enough unsolved mysteries to put fiction-writers out of business.

Here, then, is the truth that is as strange as fiction. Jacob Bowles was born in a time and a place that brought him into the midst of the battle in this country known as the Great Civil War, or the War of the Rebellion. He was of the age, and a member of a family that had a number of males of sufficient age, fit for service in that war. Thus, not only was Jacob in the war, his father and two of his brothers also served. All four of them applied for disability payments after the war – with very similar complaints. This might lead one to various speculations, and you are certainly free to reach your own conclusions. Were they genetically susceptible to the same weaknesses? Were they, perhaps, guilty of collusion? Obviously, a number of questions are possible.

I have my own suspicions concerning the validity of the claims. I can also see the necessity of the careful analysis by the boards of surgeons who must make the final decisions concerning allocating the funds of the United States government for ex-soldiers who claim to deserve the money due to their service in the war. They must make their decisions based on the information at hand, and it is not fair to hold them to the hindsight we may have in later years, where more information has come to light.

At any rate, I personally believe that Jacob Bowles was truly injured in the war to such an extent that, from the very first, he deserved a pension allotment. Instead, he spent years attempting to convince the pension board to give him anything at all. Finally, at the end, his true condition is revealed, only in time for him to enjoy a few months of income before his death. Then, instead of this being the end of the story, when his wife applies for the spousal benefits, a whole new tangled ball of yarn begins to unravel.

I have arranged the details from the sources using two different methods. First, there are the records from the Civil War Pension packet, which I have put into chronological order based on when they were processed, and have then attempted, as much as possible, to transcribe them from the original handwriting, so that they are more easily readable. This gives us the information that was available to the pension board as time went by, information that may at any given moment of time be incomplete, but that was all they had to go by in deciding whether or not to support Mr. Bowles' claim to a pension. Second, I make use of public records to establish locations and family make-up that goes beyond that available in the pension records themselves. Much of this is the stuff that genealogical research is made of – although expanded. It includes national census records, local phone directories, and local censuses.

One last insight before we begin to look at the records. I had read the documents, and was inclined to believe the story of Jacob Bowles, that he indeed was injured seriously enough in the war to warrant a pension from the United States government. But sufficient doubts remained as to what might have been done for him, both in the hospital during the war and then afterwards – certainly, doubts as to what lingering effects there may have been.

Then I had a very significant event occur in my own personal life that caused me to see things with a new set of eyes. While playing doubles ping pong, I lunged across the table to reach a ball, and crashed into an outcropping on the wall. It crushed my right arm into my ribs, and nearly knocked all the breath out of me, causing severe pain in my right ribs and soreness that developed into incredible stiffness over the next 24 hours. At night, I could barely turn over in bed, and my mobility was greatly decreased. But things gradually got better, and within a couple of weeks I had pretty much recovered from the incident. Then, after about a month, residual pain began to show up around the edges of my ribs, and in places not directly related to the original injury. I went to the chiropractor for an adjustment, and although the rib pain seemed to be decreased, I now had all my muscles around the ribs tense up – virtually going into spasm. A couple of nights later, I turned onto my left side and felt something move on the left, bringing pain in my ribs so great I could not lie on that side, and at the same time having a pain show up straight across on the other side of my ribs.

Back I went to the chiropractor, now realizing that something so minor as a ping pong injury could nearly debilitate me. Imagine, what would have been the result of a cannonball that knocked me senseless?

To shorten this long story, (which still continues to this day), I also realized the difference we have today in medical care to what Jacob Bowles would have had in the 1860s, during and after the Civil War. I went for Xrays, and it was discovered that I had a condition known as multiple myeloma, a cancer that often lodges in the bones. Obviously, I had this condition before my injury, and the ping pong incident merely served to expose a serious situation before it became more serious. Treatment was immediately begun – pain medication, drugs to combat the myeloma, chemical infusions, radiation treatment. I went from a position diagnosed as 70% marrow-involvement to a declaration of full remission at this time (which means, 0% detected involvement). Even so, my physical condition is nowhere near what it was before that fateful day. So, what then, did Jacob Bowles have to contend with, physically, not to mention trying to convince a board of skeptical physicians that he really wasn't able to perform physical labor?

Now, I must admit to you, the name "Jacob Bowles" is a deliberate fiction. Strangely enough, I will not use the truth in divulging this name to you, for that could possibly bring improper focus to living members of the family of this person, or perhaps living members of the families of relatives of this person, or any number of other connections which would otherwise be made if I used the true name of this individual.

I must also admit that, if you are truly determined to discover the actual names of the individuals involved in this story, you will probably succeed. So I ask of you, please don't bother.

And I promise you, the events and circumstances which I will outline and expound to you below are true and factual, and, I believe, at least as strange as fiction.

This, then, is a Tale of Jacob Bowles.

Discharged with Disabilities

/////////////
Civil War Records of Jacob Bowles
Transcribed from photocopies of original handwritten records.

Because Jacob Bowles applied for disability payments from the US Army following the Civil War, a wealth of paper documentation exists relative to his correspondence with the Pension Board. There is a great deal of repetition in this documentation, yet the content, to me, conveys both an historical and an informative path. I was not sure whether to include the actual historical data available from the Pension Board, but finally decided that the form of presentation was too valuable to be ignored. So I have included transcriptions of the correspondence between Jacob Bowles and the Pension Board, with underlines and bolded text to focus on the most important aspects. I would recommend that if the documentation as a whole proves too tedious, then focus on the highlighted parts of each document as providing the pertinent issues.

In the following transcriptions, I have done my best to accurately capture the original text as written by the various deponents. Unfortunately, due to a combination of poor quality, varying handwriting styles, and sometimes my own lack of expertise in military or medical matters, there are questionable words or phrases. I have attempted, in those cases, to provide something close to the original. As an example, see the entry below dated 10-04-1887, in which the short note is made that a report (on) 487 166 is "cuevled" to Attorney Chatman. It was (obviously) forwarded, or sent, or carried, or at least by some means made known to Attorney Chatman, originating, or with some origin, referring to D. Therefore, the meaning is not entirely lost, even though the exact wording is difficult to make out. Hopefully, in similar cases throughout the documentation, enough of the meaning remains so that you will be able to make some sense of the unclear words or phrases, or at least get a feel for the topics involved.

I have added underlined and bolded sections for emphasis. As mentioned above, you may want to restrict your attention to these sections.

05-01-1863
ARMY OF THE UNITED STATES Certificate of Disability for Discharge
  Private Jacob Bowles of Captain M. S. Upmann's Company, (K) of the 115th Penn. Regiment of United States Volunteers was enlisted by Capt. Dunstable of the 115th Regiment of Penn Vols. at Alleghany Penn on the <u>Eighteenth day of February 1862</u>, to serve Three years; he was born in Alleghany in the State of Pennsylvania, is <u>Twenty-Three years of age</u>, Five feet Eight inches high, Dark complexion, Hazel eyes, Black hair, and by occupation when enlisted a Shoemaker. <u>During the last two months said soldier has been unfit for duty 60 days</u>.
Station: 65th & Vine Sts.
Date: April 25th, 1863
  I certify, that I have carefully examined the said Private Jacob Bowles of Captain _____ Company, and find him <u>incapable of performing the duties of a soldier because of Scrofulous Diathesis And Constant Debility</u>.
R S Sens, Actg Surgeon.
Discharged this First day of May 1863, at Philad:Pa. R.S. Sens; Commanding the hospital.

In May of 1863, Jacob Bowles is discharged from his service in the Union Army. Based on the statements of the acting surgeon at an Army hospital, his discharge is based on a disability; therefore, without question there is a medical condition which he suffers that is significant enough to preclude his ability to serve as a soldier – indeed, he has been "unfit for duty 60 days." In all that follows, let us strive to remember this: that at the young and vibrant age of twenty-three, he was sufficiently affected during the war that he could no longer serve, exhibiting "scrofulous diathesis" (tuberculosis-like symptoms, rheumatic, swollen joints, symptoms which are often brought on by sudden shock of some kind), and "constant debility." Of course, this may be but a transient condition, but certainly we must agree that the condition is real, and at the moment, severe.

This is a key central element of all that follows. ***Jacob Bowles was discharged with a disability!***

1863 - Where is My Pension?

The "Application for Invalid Pension" is a standard form filled out by the claimant. It provides a legal framework for his claim, including personal identity and the nature of the request. Pertinent facts are included in an attempt to establish the validity of the claim. Typically, witnesses are cited.

Now it took me a while to realize that the wording does not refer to a pension that is "not valid," although the form sometimes seems to convey this impression. This is a request form for someone who is an invalid – injured – to appeal for a pension from the board.

05-02-1863
APPLICATION FOR INVALID PENSION, State of Pennsylvania, County of Philadelphia

On this Second day of May A.D. one thousand eight hundred and sixty Three, personally appeared before me, The Prothonotary of the Supreme Court of Pennsylvania within and for the County and State aforesaid, <u>Jacob Bowles, aged Twenty four years</u>, a resident of Pittsburg in the State of Pennsylvania who, being duly sworn according to law, declares that he is the identical Jacob Bowles who enlisted in the service of the United States at Pittsburg Pa. on the Eighteenth ....
Company K commanded by Capt. M. S. Upmann in the one hundred and fifteenth regiment of Pennsylvania in the war of 1861, and was <u>honorably discharged</u> on the First day of May in the year 1863; that, while in the service aforesaid, and in the line of his duty, he contracted the following – <u>injury or disability at the Battle of Fair Oaks </u>in the State of Virginia on the 31st day of May A.D. 1862, Having been <u>knocked down senseless by the concussion of a cannon</u> which was being discharged within a few feet of him, from this fall and injury from the concussion the <u>believe he contracted a disease of the kidneys and lungs which</u>

still affects him and renders him unable to earn a subsistence – He is now <u>on his way home to Pittsburg</u> Pennsylvania.

Jacob Bowles, Pittsburg, Allegheny Co, Pa

<u>Also, personally appeared</u> Hiram McGonegal and Charles C. Gold, residents of Philadelphia, persons whom I certify to be respectable and entitled to credit, and who, being by me duly sworn, say they were present and saw Jacob Bowles sign his name to the foregoing declaration; and they further <u>swear</u>, that they have every reason to believe, from the appearance of the applicant and their acquaintance with him, <u>that he is the identical person he represents himself to be</u>; and they further state, that they have no interest in the prosecution of this claim, and that the applicant is temperate and moral in his habits and has had no occupation since discharged.

It appears that immediately after, in fact, the very next day after, his certificate of discharge, Jacob Bowles applies in the county of Philadelphia, state of Pennsylvania, requesting a pension to cover his condition. He declares the reason for his claim – injury or disability in the line of duty. He refers to specific facts, and enlists the aid and testimony of witnesses.

His age is now given as twenty-four, and I suppose if we get the age within two or three years we should consider ourselves fortunate. Later on, he gives his date of birth as October, 1840, which would actually make him twenty-two at this time. At any rate, he is a young man, and if he is not in the best of health it is probably due to his injury.

05-19-1863
Certificate of Disability for Discharge, in the case of Jacob Bowles, Co. K, 115 Regt of Penna
Adjutant General's Office, May 19, 1863.
Duplicate for the Pension Officer. Saml Neck, Asst. Adjt. Genl

11-04-1863

I, Marion S. Upman, Captain of Company K 115th Regiment of Pennsylvania Volunteers hereby certify that Jacob Bowles, of Allegheny County, Pennsylvania, <u>was a private in</u> said company and whilst a private in said company in the line of his duty and in the service of the United States, <u>was at the Battle of Fair Oaks, on the 31st day of May 1862</u> was <u>stuned by a canon ball</u>, and so much <u>injured</u> thereby that he was <u>honarably discharged on the 1st day of May</u> last at Haddington hospital in Philadelphia. In witness whereof I have hereto set my hand this 4th November 1863.
M.S. Upman Capt., Comp 'K' 115th Penna Vols.

*Soon thereafter, before the end of the year, Jacob has enlisted the aid of the captain of the company in which he served, who gives testimony which confirms that Jacob Bowles was, in fact, injured during the war to such an extent that his honorable discharge stemmed from that event, and that he was discharged while still in a state of hospitalization. And yet, unless the records have been lost or misplaced, it appears that nothing was done for Mr. Bowles. Of course, the war was continuing, and it may be too much to expect that the bureaucracy would leap to attention during the waging of a massive war. But it would seem that somewhere, somehow, the processing should have begun to deal with this soldier's request. One would expect that after the end of the war, someone in the office would begin working on this soldier's behalf. Still, we see nothing whatsoever, and it is nearly **ten full years** before, once again, an attempt is made to get the wheels of the pension process into motion.*

1873 – Another Attempt

We don't see any records from the Pension Board after the first request in 1863. The best assumption is that no action was taken; effectively, the original request was ignored. Jacob Bowles does not do any immediate follow-up. Instead, he has no correspondence with the board until 1873. At that point, he reiterates his claim with an expansion of detail. He outlines his current health and his experiences during the war, as well as citing witnesses. We get the impression that his expectation is that the granting of a pension is a fait accompli.

02-07-1873   9 years and 9 months after discharge
DECLARATION FOR ORIGINAL PENSION OF AN INVALID
State of Pennsylvania, County of Elk
On this 7th day of February A.D. one thousand eight hundred and seventy-three, personally appeared before me Fred Schoening Clerk of the Court of Camnar Head, the same being a court of record within and for the county and State aforesaid, Jacob Bowles, aged 33 years, a resident of Ridgway, county of Elk, State of Pennsylvania, who, being duly sworn according to law, declares that he is married; that his wife's name was Mary A. (Pochie, Poeline), to whom he was married at Westmoreland (wife dcesd) on the 20 day of August, 1860, that he is the identical Jacob Bowles who enlisted in Captain Robert Dunstable, e(sq?), company K 115th Pa regiment, 3rd brigade (Williams) division at Pittsburg, on the 18th day of February, 1862, and was honorably discharged at Philadelphia, on the 1st day of May, 1863, that his personal description is as follows: Age, 33 years; height five feet eight inches; complexion dark; hair Black; eyes hazel; that while in the service aforesaid, and, in the line of his duty, he received the following disability, to wit:

gun shot wound in the left arm received at the battle of Fair Oaks, Va, disabling the use of the same, was first in Yorktown hospital, removed to Sugar Grove, thence to Hestonville, was treated in each of those places, There was total disability of the arm for five years. Also received stun from Cannon ball which affected lungs, that since leaving the said service, this applicant has resided in the City of Allegheny in the State of Pennsylvania, and his occupation has been Shoemaking, that prior to his entry into the service above-named, he was a man of good, sound physical health, being when enrolled, a shoemaker and of good sound health and of temperate and regular habits, that now he is partially disabled from obtaining his subsistence from manual labor in consequence of his above-named injuries received in the service of the United States; that he makes this declaration for the purpose of being placed on the invalid pension roll of the United States by reason of the disability above stated; that he hereby appoints Jon Bailey of Ridgway, Elk Co. Pa, his attorney to prosecute his claim; that he has never received nor applied for a pension; that his post office is at Ridgway, county of Elk, State of Pennsylvania; that his domicile or place of abode is on Mill Street in the village of Ridgway, Elk Co., Pa. Jacob Bowles

Attest: Jon Bailey, H. E. Young

Also personally appeared R. S. Taylor, residing at Ridgway Pa, and H.E. Young; residing at Ridgway Pa, persons whom I certify to be respectable and entitled to credit, and who, being by me duly sworn, say they were present and saw Jacob Bowles, the claimant, sign his name (or make his mark) to the foregoing declaration; that they have every reason to believe, from the appearance of said claimant and their acquaintance with him, that he is the identical person he represents himself to be; and that they have no interest in the prosecution of this claim.

R.S. Taylor; H.E. Young

This all seems to be fairly straightforward. Jacob was discharged, with an injury; he still has related injuries; he deserves a pension. But unfettered bureaucracy rises to the top!

In spite of all the previous correspondence and proof, Bowles runs head-on into disbelief that seems absolutely uncanny:

04-01-1873
Adjutant General's Office, Washington D.C., Apl 1st, 1873
Sir:

I have the honor to acknowledge the receipt from your Office of application for Pension No. 2xxxx, and to return it herewith with such information as is furnished by the files of this Office.

It appears from the Rolls on file in this Office that Jacob Bowles was enrolled on the 17th day of Feby, 1862, at Pittsburg Pa in Co. K, 115th Regiment of Penna Volunteers, to serve 3 years or during the war, and mustered into service as a Pvt on the 24th day of Feby, 1862, at Harrisburg Pa, in Co. K, 115th Regiment of Penna Volunteers, to serve 3 years, or during the war. On the Muster Roll of Co K, of that Regiment, for the months of May and June, 1862, he is reported – When last heard from in hospital at Yorktown, Same report on roll for July & Aug 1862. Sept & Oct 1862 **Absent without leave**. Same report on roll for Nov & Dec 1862. He was discharged May 1, 1863 on Surgeons Certificate of Disability. **No record of wounds**. I am, sir, very respectfully,

Your obedient servant, J.P.Martin, Asst Adj Genl

04-21-1873
WAR DEPARTMENT, Surgeon General's Office, Record and Pension Division,   Washington D.C., April 21st, 1873
(Transcript from Records)

It appears from the records filed in this Office, that Jacob Bowles, Private Co. K, 115th Reg't Penna Vols, was admitted to Hestonville General Hospital, near Phila. Pa. Aug 18, 1862, from .... for treatment for Chronic Rheumatism and was transferred March 24/63. Entered Haddington G.H. Phila. Pa. March 24, 1863 with scrofula and was discharged from service May 1st 1863 because of Scrofula. The records of Yorktown and

Harrison's Landing Va furnish no information in this case, the Regtl records are not on file. There is no such Hospital known to this office as "Sugar Grove Hospl."

By order of the Surgeon General: J.J.Woodward, Assistant Surgeon, U.S.Army, Vol. 33, No. 2602

Scrofula is "TB of the neck," and is observed most often in individuals who are immunocompromised. A question which arises is "how was the immune system compromised?" But that is a modern question. In the time of the Civil War, it is more likely that one would doubt the original health of anyone so feeble as to be affected by such a condition.

Jacob Bowles applies once again for a pension, this time in Elk County, Pennsylvania. But ten years after the events, we are reduced to the paper trail. Now the bureaucratic skepticism will have its heyday. Observe the following phrases: "it appears," "he is reported," "last heard from," "Absent without leave," "no record of wounds," "chronic rheumatism," "with scrofula," "because of scrofula," "no records," "records not on file," "no such Hospital." Ten years earlier some easy solutions might have been found; but now, a slow process of information-gathering must grind out the answers.

What information did we already have for Jacob Bowles at his discharge?
1. *He was unfit for duty 60 days up until discharge on 1 May, 1863.*
2. *He was incapable of performing the duties of a soldier due to debility.*
3. *He was honorably discharged.*
4. *He had injury or disability at the Battle of Fair Oaks, Virginia, 31 May 1862.*
5. *Knocked down senseless by the concussion of a cannon.*

6. First in Yorktown hospital.
7. Removed to Sugar Grove. (Perhaps this particular pension office doesn't have records ranging as far as Rhode Island!)
8. Thence to Hestonville.
9. Treated in each of those places.
10. Last at Haddington hospital in Philadelphia.
11. In his next declaration, in 1886 (see below), details were better outlined. He was treated at Sugar Grove Rhode Island, about one month, from there to Hestonville, from there to Haddington.

It seems obvious that the apparent periods of "absent" were most likely while he was being treated in various hospitals!

And yet, unless the records have been lost or misplaced, it appears that <u>nothing was done</u> for Mr. Bowles. (Does that sentence sound at all familiar?) This time, however, the war was over, so what is the excuse that nothing is done to follow up on Mr. Bowles' claim, other than, most likely, it is simply rejected out of hand? Mr. Bowles, in merely requesting a pension, has failed to supply the necessary catalyst to spark the response that will bring about any successful reaction from the Pension Board. And now he must endure another wait, this time sitting by for nearly <u>thirteen</u> years as nothing comes of his request.

Perhaps by now he has given up. He applied for a pension and was apparently ignored. Ten years later he applies once again, and once again nothing comes of it. Is there any reason to continue? Of course! Truth is contending with fiction now. The truth is, Jacob was injured during the war, and deserves a pension. What turns it into fiction is the response of the Pension Board.

It is possible that certain events in his life, maybe even certain new acquaintances, caused him to try once again. But this is the area of speculation, and if it is true, probably even cynical speculation. Let it suffice that, after another long lapse, Jacob Bowles once again makes his appeal to the Pension Board (this time in Erie County, the state of New York, rather than in the state of Pennsylvania).

1886 – Time Goes Drifting By

Another thirteen years have passed. Jacob Bowles is now 46 years old and living in Buffalo, New York. His claims have not substantially changed. In fact, nothing but his age has substantially changed. Still, he continues to hope that the evaluation of the Board will change.

01-27-1886

DECLARATION FOR ORIGINAL INVALID PENSION, State of New York, County of Erie

On this 27 day of January, A.D. one thousand eight hundred and eighty-six personally appeared before me, Clerk of the County Court, a court of record within and for the county and State aforesaid, Jacob Bowles, aged 46 years, a resident of the City of Buffalo county of Erie State of New York, who, being duly sworn according to law, declares that he is the identical Jacob Bowles, who was enrolled on the 18 day of February, 1862, in company K of the 115th regiment of Penna Vols, commanded by M. S. Upmann, and was honorably discharged in Philadelphia on the 1 day of May, 1863; that his personal description is as follows: Age, 46 years; height, 5 feet 8 inches; complexion dark; hair black; eyes hazel. That while a member of the organization aforesaid, in the service and in the line of his duty at Fair Oaks, in the State of Virginia on or about the First day of June, 1862, he was stunned by a cannon shot, affecting the entire system stopping the circulation of blood – the results of which were apparent for over **4 years** after the occurrence, causing general debility during that period – and the effects are still apparent in the spine – being weak and painfull. That he was treated in hospitals as follows: at Sugar Grove Rhode Island about one month. sent from there to Philadelphia Hestonville Hospital. remained there broken up from there to Haddington Hospital. That he has not been employed in the military or naval service otherwise than as stated above Except on <u>detached service in Hospital</u>. That since leaving the service this applicant has resided in the City of Allegheny in the State of Penna, and his <u>occupation has been that of a coat & shoe dealer</u>. That prior to his entry into the service above named he was a man of good, sound physical health, being when enrolled a <u>shoemaker</u>. That he is now <u>partially disabled</u> from obtaining his subsistence by manual labor by reason of his injuries, above described,<u> received in the service of the United States;</u> and he therefore makes this declaration for the purpose of being placed on the invalid pension-roll of the United States.

    He hereby appoints James W. Chatman of Buffalo, State of New York, his true and lawful attorney to prosecute his claim. That he has not received nor applied for a pension. That his Post Office Address is 30 Exchange St, Buffalo, county of Erie, State of New York.   Claimant's signature: Jacob Bowles Attest: John J. Aeschbach; James Oswald

Of course, by this time, one might wonder if a pension for disability is really necessary. After all, this soldier has carried on for more than twenty-two years since being discharged, and apparently has been able to earn his living. Indeed, as it shall become apparent, he has not only earned a living but has raised a family. So he is obviously not completely impaired. Then what is the extent of his disability? Exactly how does it affect his ability to do manual labor?

Also, we should note that now Mr. Bowles has enlisted the services of an attorney – a definite indication of the increasing seriousness of his efforts. This time, finally, there is a response from the Pension Board – and a medical examination is ordered.

02-11-1886

Feb 11/86 - (client/climb) (hr/for) Hon. J.B.Wabar for offcr's or comrades & Surg's test as to –ngen & Med or other competent test as to (centurennces).

02-14-1886

Feb 14/86 – Atty J.W.C. Med Ex Bd, **Buffalo**, NY.

02-24-1886

ORIGINAL (For a Board)   Claim No. 2xxxx

Name of the claimant, <u>Jacob Bowles</u>

Rank, Pv, Company K, Regiment 115 Pa V

Post-office address, 33 Exchange St, Buffalo, NY.

Buffalo, Erie, New York.

Date of examination Feb 24, 1886

We hereby certify that in compliance with the requirements of the law we have <u>carefully examined</u> this applicant, who claims that while in the service of the United States at or near a place named Fair Oaks, and while in line of duty, on or about the ...... day of Spring, 1862, he incurred <u>affection of spine result of concussion of cannonball</u> and that in consequence thereof he is .... <u>disabled for earning his subsistence by manual labor</u>. His pulse-rate is 85 per minute; his respiration 17; his temperature 98 2/5, his height is 5 feet and 8 inches; he weighs 188 pounds, and states that he is <u>45 years of age</u>.

Touching the cause and degree of the disability for which he claims a pension, he makes the following statement: claims pain in small of back troubles him more recently with changes of weather – <u>was in military hospital in service</u>.

The examination reveals the following objective facts in support of his statements: there is **<u>no paralysis or impaired or abnormal sensation – he is a powerfully muscled, well nourished, high colored man, spinal curvatures and flexibility unimpaired, no tenderness on pressure, no scar or</u>**

other objective signs of injury.

No Drs

From the existing condition and the history of this claimant, as stated by himself, it is, in our judgment, …………... probable that the disability was incurred in the service as he claims, and that it has not been aggravated or prolonged by vicious habits. He is, in our opinion, entitled to a 0 rating for the disability caused by affection of spine, ----- for that caused by ---
--------, and --------- for that caused by --------, the sum of which aggregates 0.

Charles Cacy, Pres, P Wrunt Peyma Secy, F W Abbott, Treas.

Jacob Bowles might wish at this time that he had never re-opened this pension can of worms. His first medical exam is a disaster. It sounds like he is the sort of ex-college athlete you'd like to recruit as a player for your local rugby team, and then smugly sit back, ready to take on all comers. At the age of forty-five he is "powerfully muscled, well-nourished, high-colored, with unimpaired bones and flexibility, impervious to pain and with no apparent history of injury." Superman has come to visit us from another planet! Not only that, but the Physicians' Board says that even though it is "probable that the disability was incurred in the service," it is effectively not a big enough deal to warrant disability payments!

Here, then, is an incredible puzzle. Clearly, Jacob Bowles perceives himself as seriously disabled due to his tour of duty in the Union Army. He has struggled to earn his livelihood over the past twenty-some odd years, periodically applying to the Pension Board for assistance. I am convinced that his own self-evaluation is that he hasn't the necessary strength or stamina to pursue a normal career that involves physical labor. And yet, whenever a spot check of his physical health is done, at a given moment on a given day, at least as measured by the normal *metrics such as pulse, respiration, weight, and appearance, he is declared to be in the **finest possible condition**.*

Is it any wonder that nothing comes of his request?

Over the next few years:

02-20-1888
ORIGINAL INVALID CLAIM
Soldier Jacob Bowles, PO Buffalo, 33 Exchange St, Erie NY.
Pvt, Company K, Regiment 115 Pen Vol Inf
REJECTED FEB 20, 1888
Name James W. Chatman, Buffalo, NY
Approved – Rejection
Submitted Jrry, Feb 6, 1888   J.W.Swohn, Examiner
Rejected on the ground of Claimants failure after a reasonable time, and due notification, to furnish the necessary evidence to establish the claim.
Feb 12, 88   D.Birtwell, Legal Receiver
Feby 17, 1888 Re-reviewer
Enlisted Feby 17, 1862, mustered 1862,
Discharged May 1, 1863,
Declaration filed May 8, 1863, Feby 10, 1873, Feby 2, 1886
BASIS OF CLAIM: In declaration filed May 8, 1863 claimant alleges that on or about May 31, 1862, he received an injury resulting diseases of kidneys & lungs, In declaration filed Feby 10, 78, gun shot wound left arm & diseases of lungs, results of injury. In declaration filed February 2, 1886 he was stuned by a cannon shot resulting in non-circulation of blood. General debility – affecting spinal.

02-28-1888   Alg odrets notified claim rejected

Feb 28 Algy Chatman Notified Claim Rejected – D

He has encountered a tragedy! The response by the Pension Board is even less helpful than their previous lack of response and indifference to Mr. Bowles' claim. Instead of having doors open, it appears that a door has closed. REJECTED! Not only that, but the board appears to lay the burden of rejection on Jacob – "failure after a reasonable time, and due notification, to furnish the necessary evidence to establish the claim."

Well, what more evidence do they need than what has already been provided since his discharge? Don't they already know that he was discharged from service due to disabilities brought on by his time of service? Or at least, based on the paper trail we have seen, they should. They have the testimony of Captain Upmann. But, unfortunately, the physical exam just seems to show that the past is past, and that at present, Jacob Bowles has no need whatsoever of government assistance. Apparently, the Disability Bureau is looking for other sources of confirmation: records of private doctors, testimony of other witnesses, etc. Perhaps if Jacob Bowles or his attorney had realized this earlier, they could have been more effective.

Is anything to be done, or has a dead end been reached? Is there anything that can convince a board of physicians that, perhaps, a single spot check on a given day might not really expose the true nature of Mr. Bowles' disability? Will the testimony of another physician be of any use, perhaps one who can give evidence that persists over time, rather than the evidence of a single, random office checkup? Or is this a lost cause? Don't the very nature of Mr. Bowles' requests now mitigate against his ability to convince anyone in authority that he has a case? After all, he has rather haphazardly tossed a request toward the Pension Board every ten years or so, and when his request is ignored or rejected, he simply disappears for a while.

We wait another seven years before there is a successive attempt to convince someone, anyone, that Jacob Bowles deserves a pension, to assist him in his living expenses.

1895 – Nobody Believes Me

Another seven years have passed since Jacob Bowles' last interaction with the Pension Board. His standard "Invalid Claim" forms having already been submitted, he now submits evidence from a practicing physician. This is a new approach for him. He has made his own claims, expecting that would be sufficient for validation of his condition. Perhaps it is beginning to dawn on him that his frustrations might outweigh his progress.

09-03-1895

MEDICAL EVIDENCE. Affidavit of Cecil A. Keller, MD, #1223 Jefferson St, Buffalo, NY.

Claim of Jacob Bowles, Co K 115th Regt Pa

Vol Inf No. of claim 2x,xxx

for Original Invalid Pension, Filed by W.H. Peck, Room 9, Williams Block, Buffalo, NY.

PHYSICIAN'S AFFIDAVIT State of New York, County of Erie, SS: In the Pension Claim No. 2x,xxx of Jacob Bowles, late of Co. K 115th Regt Pa Vol Inf. Personally came before me, a Corn'r of Deeds, Buffalo, NY, in and for the aforesaid County and State, Cecil A. Keller, a citizen of Buffalo NY, whose Post Office address is 1223 Jefferson St, Buffalo, NY, well known to me to be reputable and entitled to credit, and who, being duly sworn, declared in relation to the aforesaid case as follows: That he is a Practicing Physician, and that he has been acquainted with said soldier for about 2 ¼ years, and that:

I meet the above Jacob Bowle for the first time in May 1893 when called to attend him as a patient I found him in a low state of vitality – suffering with a pain in the lower jaw and left hip and leg. he was confined to his house and bed at the time. I saw him many time every month until the following March 1894 when I opperated (assisted by Dr. B.C.Johnson & Dr L.H.Lynor of Buffalo N.Y.) on his lower jaw and removed a quantity of necrosed bone by cutting in from the lower and outer side of his face. In a few months the wound heald leaving a bad scar. He then felt a little better for two or three mo. When he again consulted me I found his left leg getting worse. A large swelling appeared just below the hip. In March 1895 I again operated assisted by Dr. B.C. Johnson & Dr. Harry Ruth, we opened the leg just below the buttock down to the bone and removed a large amount of dead & necrosed bone. Owing to his low vitality we were obliged to stop the operation and administer stimulant to save his life. There is still a fistula leading to the remaining dead bone of the femur which discharges continuously. From his family and personal history I believe the necrosed (or dead bone) **was caused by his low state of vitality brought on by exposure and shock while in the late war.** The above Jacob Bowle has been under my personal care for over two years. I have seen at my office or his house every month during this time. At no time has he been able to do any manual labor and his outlook for a recovery are very poor. This affidavit was written by me on this 30th day of August 1895 from my own personal knowledge and belief and in making the same I was not aided or prompted by any other person.

He further declares that he has been a practitioner of medicine for Nine years, and that he has no interest, either direct or indirect, in the prosecution of this claim.

Cecil A. Keller.

Sworn to and subscribed before me this 3rd day of September, A.D. 1895.

John M. Looney, Com'r of Deeds for Buffalo, N.Y.

It is now 1895, some thirty years after the war, the original injuries and the medical discharge. What kind of an impact does 30 years have? All of life has changed. From a young man, the petitioner has become at least middle-aged; his family and lifestyle have changed immeasurably. In a sense, he is no longer the man who was first discharged from service. But still he plods on. This is an incredible example of tenacity.

Finally, the testimony of a private physician is included. Jacob Bowles has seen a number of things change by this time. Apparently, the "hidden" internal conditions of physical weakness which had persisted since his time in the service have finally manifested themselves in the form of dead tissue, dead bone, and a low state of vitality. He enlists the aid of the physician who has now dealt with these issues to testify as to his current physical condition. Also, he has appointed a different attorney to handle his case.

Perhaps this has been his problem all along. At first, he naïvely applied as an individual, assuming that his case was so transparently true that the Board would simply acknowledge his need and initiate his pension. Later, after making another appeal, he appoints an attorney to prosecute his claim, but there is apparently no follow-up. Most likely, it is his new attorney who has urged him to include the testimony of his physician when he makes his claim. At any rate, what we see in the correspondence to follow is that he no longer lets the ball drop, but instead pursues the issue until it reaches a conclusion.

12-18-1895   (3 months later)
SURGEON'S CERTIFICATE in case of Jacob Bowles, Co. K
115 Reg't Pa Inf,
Applicant for Orig No. 2xxxx. Date of Examination Dec. 18,
1895,
W H Hinesn, J.B. Stiggs, M. Talbot, **Post office Lockport**,
County Majnon, New York.
Orig. Pension Claim No. 2xxxx. Jacob Bowles; Rank, Priv;
Company K, 115 Regt, Pa Inf, Lockport NY, 44 Spruce St,
Buffalo NY, Dec 18, 1895.
        We hereby certify that in compliance with the
requirements of the law we have carefully examined this
applicant, who states that he is suffering from the following
disability, incurred in the service, viz., Lung & Kidney trouble,
GS wound of left arm affecton of spine general (ochar) poor

circulation of blood. General debility. Weakness of back. (orsinar) of bowels, Rheumatism Necrosis of Lower Jaw and left thigh. GS wound of right arm, and a stun from cannon ball.

   Upon examination we find the following objective conditions: Pulse rate, 80; respiration, 20; temperature 98 2/5; height 5 feet 8 inches; weight, 184 pounds; age, 55 years. We found heart & lungs in normal condition. Apex brat ½ inch below nipple and one inch to right. Liver & spleen normal. No evidence of general debility. Claimant is well nourished. Skin clear. We found no disease of bowels. No evidence of Rheumatism. No evidence of drainar of back or spine. or Kidney, Urine normal. We found a GS wound of right arm two inches below elbow on radial side. Skin normal. Scar is not adherent or dragging. No exit. no loss of tissue or motion. We find a large scar on right lower jaw. We find considerable loss of bone and tissue due to necrosis and has been operated upon. Scar is modular, adherent tender & dragging. Wound has entirely healed. We found a discharging wound of left thigh, posterior middle third. Has been operated on for necrosis. Measurement of leg 24 in of right leg 21 ½ covered is painful and evidence of necrosis still exists. There is loss of tissue and claimant walks lame.

   W.H. Hodson   J.B.Stiggs   M. Talbot

No evidence of injury from cannon ball. There is no evidence of vicious habits. Claimant cannot perform manual labor. We found no other disability. Rating Lower Jaw 4/18. left thigh 17/18.

   At least this time the surgeons' board found evidence of a gun-shot wound, even if the cannon ball is still AWOL! I still wonder what the previous surgeons were looking for when they found "no scar or other objective signs of injury."

   So, now Jacob Bowles is found to be disabled by a certified board of surgeons. Notice the strong statement: "Claimant cannot perform manual labor." But alas! His disability seems due to his most recent visits to the doctor, and not his tour of duty as a soldier. Yes, his jaw is rated at 4 out of 18, and his left thigh at 17 out of 18 – but are those problems due to injuries sustained during the war? Without any such determination, the final outcome is no better than it would have been had Jacob Bowles been declared in the peak of health.

03-11-1896
ORIGINAL INVALID CLAIM No. 2x,xxx
Soldier, Jacob Bowles, 44 Spruce St, Buffalo, Erie, NY
Pvt, Co K, Regiment 115 Pa Vol Inf, commencing May 2, 1863
REJECTED
Recognized Attorney: Name W.H. Peck, PO Buffalo NY,
Fee $10, Agent is to pay. Articles filed none.
Approvals: Approved for general disability, Submitted for adm, Feby 26, 1896,

                         J.F. Stewart Examiner
Approved for: Rejection of alleged disease and resulting disease of kidneys and lungs of claimant. Wound of left arm no notable disability therefrom since date of discharge, and alleged cannon shot resulting in non circulation of blood, general debility and affectation of spine rejected, no notable disability shown therefrom since date of filing as per action.
        Med. Ref. Williams, Legal Reviewer, Mch 11, 1896.
Coleman, Med. Ex'r W.W.F. Med. Reviewer, Mch 7, 1896.
        Thos Featherstone. DO
Important Dates: (?Houchars Canise Aug. 24, 1895. Y. Fritz.?)

04-06-1896
GENERAL AFFIDAVIT. State of New York, County of Erie, SS: in the matter of Claim for original invalid pension No. 2x,xxx of Jacob Bowles, Co. K, 115th Regt, Pa Inf Vols. On this 6 day of April, A.D. 1896, personally appeared before me, a Notary Public in and for the aforesaid County, duly authorized to administer oaths, Jacob Bowles, aged 55 years, a resident of

Buffalo, in the County of Erie and State of New York, whose Post Office address is 44 Spruce St, Buffalo, NY, well known to me to be reputable and entitled to credit, and who, being duly sworn, declares in relation to the aforesaid case as follows:

I am the claimant above named. My claim for pension was recently rejected by the Pension Bureau – for causes, or reasons, contained in a letter from the Pension Bureau under date of March 24 1896. I herewith submit a medical affadavit from my physician, and **request another examination** before some **other board** to determine my right to a pension. I am **very much dissatisfied** with the adverse decision of the Pension Bureau and know that <u>I am entitled to a pension</u> which the law and evidence in the claim.

I made the above statement to William W. Peck in his office in Buffalo NY, April 6 1896 and he reduced the same to writing in my presence, and from my oral statements then and there made to him. In reading the same, I was not made by any other person in any manner whatsoever.

X Jacob Bowles

Perhaps Jacob has been talking to other ex-soldiers about their dealings with the Pension Board, and has discovered that it is not so much merit that gets a result, but rather having the right representation and applying to the specific locations that are most likely to give a favorable response. Also, he seems to have realized the value of persistence – refusing to take "no" for an answer, but rather immediately submitting a new claim whenever a claim is rejected.

Here, he shows his determination to beat the system. If one particular board of surgeons cannot see fit to declare him deserving of a pension, perhaps there is another board which is not so unresponsive. Surely there must be someone, somewhere, who will realize and recognize his plight!

04-06-1896

MEDICAL EVIDENCE. Affidavit of Cecil A. Keller, MD Claim of Jacob Bowles, Co K 115th Regt Pa Vol Inf No. of claim 2x,xxx for Original Invalid Pension, Filed by W.H. Peck, Room 9, Williams Block, Buffalo, NY.

PHYSICIAN'S AFFIDAVIT State of New York, County of Erie, SS: In the Pension Claim No. 2x,xxx of Jacob Bowles, late of Co. K 115th Regt Pa Vol Inf. Personally came before me, a Notary Public, in and for the aforesaid County and State, <u>Cecil A. Keller M.D.</u>, a citizen of Buffalo NY, whose Post Office address is 1223 Jefferson St, Buffalo, NY, <u>well known to me to be reputable and entitled to credit</u>, and who, being duly sworn, declared in relation to the aforesaid case as follows:

I have been <u>personally acquainted</u> with Mr. Jacob Bowle for about 2 ¾ years. I meet him for the first time in May 1893 when called to <u>attend him as a patient</u> I found him in a <u>low state of vitality</u> – suffering with pain in the lower jaw and left hip and leg. he was <u>confined to his house and bed</u> at the time. I saw him many time every month until the following March, 1894 when I operated (assisted by Dr. B.C.Johnson & Dr L.H.Lynor of Buffalo) on his lower jaw and removed a quantity of necrosed bone by cutting in from the lower and outer side of his face. In a few months the wound healed leaving a bad scar. He then felt a little better for two or three mo. When he consulted me again I found his left leg worse. A large swelling appeared just below the hip. In March 1895 I again operated assisted by Dr. B.C. Johnson & Dr. H. Ruth. We opened the leg just below the buttock down to the bone and removed a large amount of dead bone. Owing to his <u>low state of vitality</u> we were obliged to stop the operation and administer stimulants to save his life. There is still a fistula leading to the remaining dead bone of the femur which discharges constantly. <u>From his family and personal history I believe the necrosed (or dead bone) was caused by his low state of vitality</u> **brought on by exposure and shock while in the late war.** The above Jacob Bowle has been <u>under my personal care for over two and one half years</u>. I have seen him at my office or his house every month during this time. <u>At no time has he been able to do any manual labor and his outlook for a recovery are very poor.</u> This affidavit was written by me on this 3 day of April 1896 from my own personal knowledge and belief and in making the same I was not aided or prompted by any other person.

He further declares that he has been a practitioner of medicine for 8 years, and that he has no interest, either direct or indirect, in the prosecution of this claim.

Cecil A. Keller M. D.

Sworn to and subscribed before me this 6 day of April, A.D. 1896. M. E. Peck, Notary Public

07-17-1896

Medical Division, Bureau of Pensions, Washington, D.C. July 17, 1896

No. Claim 2xxxx, Jacob Bowles, Co. K, 115 Reg't Pa Inf. Respectfully returned to the Chief of the Middle Division with the opinion that the affidavit referred to in his slip of the 13 inst **does not warrant any change** <u>of action or reopening of the rejected claim; for the reason that the disabilities therein described have</u> **not been shown to have been due to the service**<u>, nor is it believed that such connection is</u> **susceptible of proof**.

J.K. Boude   Approved   Thos. Featherstone. Holr.

Great! Now we're encountering the attitude that even if papers are submitted, or doctor's testimony is introduced, or an examination made by a board of physicians, the attempt will be futile. Indeed, the attitude is "nor is it believed that such connection is susceptible of proof." That is, no matter what is found, there will never be a way of proving it is a result of anything that happened during the war!

07-21-1896
96, July 21, Atty Peck notice as per secty of Med Refer of July 17/98. F.Y.S.

07-26-1896
Department of the Interior, Bureau of Pensions, Washington D.C. July 26, 1896
No. 2x,xxx, Jacob Bowles, Co. K, 115 Reg't Pa Inf. Date of filing May 8, 1863.
Date of rejection July 18, 1888.
Cause of Rejection – Failure to complete DC.
Abstract of testimony to reopen – Has furnished evidence and has been examined.
J.F. Stewart, Examiner.　　　　　　G. Ribble, Chief of Div.

The months are still passing by. No progress is apparent. All efforts appear futile. And yet, the tone of the correspondence from the Pension Board seems to take on a new sense. Somehow, behind the scenes, something seems to be changing!

Probably on the advice of his attorney, Jacob Bowles gathers together and presents testimony from other soldiers in his division. Something seems to be pulling together.

04-06-1897
97 Apr 6 to sur. div for test F.Y.S.

09-04-1897
Sept 4/97 Atty Peck names and address of officers and comrades. F.Y.S.

02-06-1898

Jacob F. Bowles ~~33 Exchange St, Buffalo, NY.~~ 44 Spruce St,
Buffalo NY

Priv. K 115 Pa Inf   9/26/19 MOR   ~~REJECTED~~

Enlisted Feb 18, 1862.   Discharged May 1, 1863

Application filed Feby 1886

Alleges: spine mate pimbral caused by concussion of cannon
ball.   REJECTED

Attorney: James M. Chatman, Buffalo, NY   REJECTED

11-09-1898

ADDITIONAL EVIDENCE. Proof of Disability –

Claim of Jacob Bowles, Co. K. 115th Regt Pa Vol Infty, No.
2xxxx

Filed by W.H. Peck, Room 9, Williams Block, Buffalo, NY.

Proof of Disability, State of Colorado, County of Arapahoe, SS:
On this 9 day of Nov, A.D. 1898, personally appeared before me,
a Dep Co Clerk in and for the aforesaid County, duly authorized
to administer oaths, xM.S. Upman aged 64 years, a resident of
Denver in the County of Arapahoe and State of Colorado, who
being duly sworn according to law, state that …….. acquainted
with Jacob Bowles, applicant for Invalid Pension, and know the
said Jacob Bowles to be the identical person of that name who
enlisted, or volunteered, as a private in Company K. 115
Regiment of Pa. Infty. Vols, and who was discharged.

That the same Jacob Bowles, while in the line of his duty,
at or near Fair Oaks in the State of Virginia did, on or about the -
----- day of May, 1862, become disabled in the following
manner, viz.: While in battle, and line of duty the said soldier
was injured by being thrown to the ground, in some manner, and
from some cause, and severely injured and stunned. He was
injured so seriously that he was unable to do duty, and was sent
away to a hospital for treatment, and he did not return to his
company again for service, and I understand that he was
discharged for disability.

That the facts stated are **personally known** to the affiant by reason of: I being 1<u>st</u> <u>Lieut and in command over at the time</u> the (catpdone hury disinbeirce the ....) at the time, and **I was present when he was injured**. He seemed to be <u>numbed or partially paralized,</u> for he did not have the free use of his physical person. In the excitement of the battle, I am unable to say what the cause of the injury was, but am sure that it was done through no fault or improper conduct of soldier. <u>I am certain as to his disability, for he was sent away to the hospital the next day, in or amal I saw him when he was placed on board the (bor. to gr unay). Up to the time, soldier was a strong and able bodied man, and performed his duty well and faithfully.</u>

And deponent further states that he was well acquainted with the claimant, <u>having known him for at least from enlistment</u>, and further, that my knowledge of the facts above stated were derived from said acquaintance, and from having served as <u>Captain of Company K,</u> of the 115th Regiment of Pa. Infty Volunteers, from the 31 day of May, 1862 (<u>I arrived as Louft in Oct 1862</u>) to the day of February, 1864. And deponent further states that the claimant was a sound and able-bodied man at and prior to enlistment, so far as he knew, and that he is totally disinterested in this claim. Post office address of affiant is 3022 West 23rd St, Denver, Colorado.
x M.S. Upman, Capt. Co K, PV.

State of Colorado, County of Arapahoe, SS: Sworn to and subscribed before me this day by the aforenamed affiant, and I certify that I read said affidavit to said affiant, and acquainted him with its contents before he executed the same. I further certify that I am in nowise interested in said case, nor am I concerned in its prosecution; and that said affiant is personally known to me and that he is a credible person.N.S. Phistn, Dep Co Clerk

01-14-1899

ADDITIONAL EVIDENCE. Proof of Disability –

Claim of Jacob Bowles, Co. K. 115th Regt Pa Vol Infty, No. 2xxxx

Filed by W.H. Peck, Room 9, Williams Block, Buffalo, NY.

Proof of Disability, State of Pennsylvania, County of Allegheny, SS: On this 14 day of Jan, A.D. 1899, personally appeared before me, a Clerk of Court in and for the aforesaid County, duly authorized to administer oaths, (1)Frank G. Upman, aged 53 years, a resident of Castle Shannon in the County of Allegheny and State of Penna, duly sworn according to law, state that he is acquainted with Jacob Bowles, applicant for Invalid Pension, and know the said Jacob Bowles to be the identical person of that name who enlisted, or volunteered, as a private in Company K. 115 Regiment of Pa. Infty. Vols.

That the same Jacob Bowles, while in the line of his duty, at or near Fair Oaks in the State of Virginia did, on or about the ---- day of May, 1862 become disabled in the following manner, viz.: While in battle and line of duty, the said soldier was injured by being knocked down in some manner and **severely injured, and stuned.** he was taken to the rear, and being injured so severely was sent away to a hospital for treatment and he **did not return to his company again for duty,** and I believe that he was discharged for injuries received at the battle of Fair Oaks.

That the facts stated are personally known to the affiant by reason of: being Second Lieut and I was in the battle of Fair Oaks Va, and saw the said Jacob Bowles fall to the ground and spoke to him. He appeared to be paralyzed and did not have the use of his physical powers, and could not get up or help himself and was carried to the rear. The next day he was placed on board of a car and sent to a hospital. Jacob Bowles up to this time was a good soldier, was strong and active, and performed all his duties well and faithfully.

And deponent further states that he is well acquainted with the claimant, having known him for at least 38 years, and further, that the knowledge of the facts above stated were derived from said acquaintance, and from having served as <u>Lieutenant of Company K,</u> of the 115th Regiment of Pennsylvania Volunteers, <u>from the 3rd day of September 1861 to the 30th day of March, 1865</u>. And deponent further states that the claimant was a sound and able-bodied man at and prior to enlistment, so far as he knew, and that he is totally disinterested in this claim. Post office address of affiant is Court Shannon, Allegheny Co., Pennsylvania.

(1) Frank G. Upman

State of Pennsylvania, County of Allegheny, SS: Sworn to and subscribed before me this day by the aforenamed affiant, and I certify that I read said affidavit to said affiant, and acquainted him with its contents before he executed the same. I further certify that I am in nowise interested in said case, nor am I concerned in its prosecution; and that said affiant is personally known to me and that he is a credible person.

Geo W. Miller, Clerk of Court

Three years have passed and now the eyewitness accounts of two superior officers have been introduced into evidence. The wheels of bureaucracy are grinding inexorably toward something. Think of it! Jacob Bowles was discharged at the age of 23 years of age, in May of 1863. He was "unfit for duty" and was declared incapable of performing the duties of a soldier because of Scrofulous Diatheses and Constant Debility. And yet now, 36 years later, 60 years old, he is barely beginning to scratch the surface of a response from the authorities, even with two eyewitness accounts and the help of a lawyer and the testimony of an attending physician.

06-09-1899

June 9/99 Atty Peck for evidence <u>showing existence of disabilities and that same is due to service</u>. F.T.F.

06-23-1899

MEDICAL EVIDENCE. No. 2x,xxx, Jacob Bowles, Co K 115th Regt Pa Inf Vols.,

Nature of claim Original Invalid

Affidavit of Cecil A. Keller, MD

Filed by W.H. Peck, Room 9, Williams Block, Buffalo, NY.

PHYSICIAN'S AFFIDAVIT State of New York, County of Erie, SS: In the Pension Claim No. 2x,xxx of Jacob Bowles, late of Co. K 115th Regt Pa Vol Inf. Personally came before me, a Notary Public, in and for the aforesaid County and State, Cecil A. Keller M.D., a citizen of Buffalo NY, whose Post Office address is 1223 Jefferson St, Buffalo, NY, well known to me to be reputable and entitled to credit, and who, being duly sworn, declared in relation to the aforesaid case as follows:

I have been personally acquainted with Mr. Jacob Bowle 7 ½ years. He came to my office in 1892 suffering with great pain in lower left jaw. I found him in a very low state of vitality. He also had pain in his left leg & hip. He was soon thereafter confined to his house and bed. I saw him many times at my and his home until the following March, 1894 when I operated (assisted by B. C. Johnson & S.H. Lynde of Buffalo) on his lower jaw and removed a large quantity of necrosed bone. In a few months the wound healed leaving a bad scar on the jaw. He then felt a little better for the next 3 months. When he again consulted me I found his left leg worse. A large swelling appeared just below the hip. In March 1895 I again operated assisted Dr. B.C. Johnson & Dr. Harry Ruth. We opened the leg just below buttock down to the bone. We removed a large amount of dead and necrosed bone. Owen to his low vitality were we were obliged to stop operation and admister stimulant to save his life. A fistula remained for a long time leading to the diseased bone. I am still attending Jacob Bowles to the present time. He has never been able to do any manuel since 1893. From his personal and family history I believe necrosed was caused by his low state of vitality **brought on** by exposure and shock **while in the war of the Rebellion**. The above Jacob

Bowle has been under my personal care for six years. I have seen him at my office or his hom nearly every month during this time. <u>At no time has he been able to do any manual labor</u>. This affidavit was written by me on this 20th day of June 1899 from my own personal knowledge and belief and in making the same I was not aided or prompted by any other person. I further declare that I have been a practicing physician for eleven years.

He further declares that he has been a practitioner of medicine for Eleven years, and that he has no interest, either direct or indirect, in the prosecution of this claim.

Cecil A. Keller M. D.

Sworn to and subscribed before me this 23rd day of June, A.D. 1899.   M. E. Peck,   Notary Public

12-18-1900 Hon. D. S. Alexander that evidence file since rejection **will not reopen** claim. F.T.F.

One and a half years later, still rejected, and so he brings in another physician. This is a major battle!

1901 - Protests

Let's examine what Jacob Bowles has submitted so far. In 1863, upon his discharge, being roughly 22-24 years of age, he applied for a pension using the standard form, as well as providing a testimony of the captain of his company as witness. In 1873, at the age of 33, he submits another standard form with more detail concerning his condition. The Board rejects his request. In 1886, at the age of 46, he goes through the same process. This time, he manages to secure a physicians' exam from the board at Buffalo. His condition is rated superb. Finally, in 1895, he solicits the testimony of a private physician. Three months later, he is granted the opportunity for another examination. Although the board sympathises with his condition, his claim is rejected with respect to whether the injuries are war-related. Jacob continues to request further examinations. He submits another private physician's affidavit. He submits the testimonies of two of his superior officers during his time of service. He adds another private physician's affidavit. By now, he must be realizing that the deck is stacked against him. So, rather than simply "requesting" action, he now begins to protest and complain.

01-25-1901
PHYSICIAN'S AFFIDAVIT, State of New York, County of Erie, SS:
In the pension claim No. 2x,xxx: of Jacob Bowle, late of Co. K. 115th Reg't. Pa. Vol. Infty., Personally came before me, a Com'r of Deeds, in and for the aforesaid County and State Frank R. Glaston, M.D., a citizen of Buffalo NY, whose Post-Office address is 634 Michigan St., well known to me to be reputable and entitled to credit, and who, being duly sworn, declares in relation to the aforesaid case as follows:

That he is a Practicing Physician, and that he has been acquainted with said soldier for about 4 years, and that he has treated Mr. Jacob Bowles at various times since then for muscular rheumatism, kidney trouble, nasal catarrh (hypertrophie) (croenk) heart action. I first treated him Aug 10, 1900 up to and including the present time. Mr. Bowles has been suffering and still is suffering from a great deal of pain in back, chest, arms, &tc (due to muscular rheumatism which together with his other ailments has incapacitated him from performing his usual vocation. He is also suffering from dizziness & general weakness as a result of weak heart action. Mr Bowle has had **severe attacks of acute nephritis, the the urine being high colored, highly acid & containing small amounts of albumen**.

Frank R. Glaston

01-28-1901
General law.   GENERAL AFFIDAVIT
State of New York, County of Erie, SS: In the matter of claim for original invalid pension No. 2x,xxx of Jacob Bowles, Co. K. 115th Regt. Pa. Vol. Inf.
On this 28" day of January, A.D. 1901, personally appeared before ma, a Com'r of Deeds in and for the aforesaid County, duly authorized to administer oaths, Jacob Bowles, aged 60 years, a resident of Buffalo, in the County of Erie and State of New York, whose Post-office address is 27 Spruce St, Buffalo, NY., well known to me to be reputable and entitled to credit, and who, being duly sworn, declares in relation to the aforesaid case as follows:

I am the claimant above named. This claim was recently rejected on the ground that I had not been disabled in a pensionable degree since filing the claim, from the diseases and disabilities alleged.

That this decision is unjust, and is not true, for I am and have been greatly disabled from said causes since this incurred and since disability is increasing constantly, but slowly. So that for the first year and more I have been

partially unable to do manual labor. I submit the testimony of a physician who has treated me for some time and who is now treating me for said diseases and I respectfully request that I be favored with an early order to appear before the medical board at Springville, Even for W.T. to determine my right to said pension, for I know that I am entitled under the law 7 the facts: I do not know any member of the Springville, Sein Co. WT medical board. Jacob Bowles

02-21-1901 Atty Peck evidence filed not sufficient to reopen. F.T.F.

04-01-1901 Atty Peck for origin of condit of rheum and heart disease. F.T.F.

05-??-1901 (received 05-16-1901)
PHYSICIAN'S AFFIDAVIT,
State of New York, County of Erie, SS:
In the pension claim No. 2x,xxx: of Jacob Bowle, late of Co. K. 115th Reg't. Pa. Vol. Infty., Personally came before me, a Notary Public, in and for the aforesaid County and State Frank R. Glaston, a citizen of Buffalo NY, whose Post-Office address is 634 Michigan, well known to me to be reputable and entitled to credit, and who, being duly sworn, declares in relation to the aforesaid case as follows:

That he is a Practicing Physician and that he has been acquainted with said soldier for about 4 years, and that he treated Mr. Jacob Bowles at various times since Aug 10 1900 & since then & including the present time (see my affidavit of Jan 25, 1901) but as the information therein contained was deemed indefinite I have again carefully examined Mr. Jacob Bowle especially with reference to his heart action which is irregular intermittent & subject to a great change as regards the frequency of its action. Several days ago his pulse was 68. After having him walk 4 times across the room & return his pulse was 112 & the character of the beat very poor – irregular & intermittent.

Last evening after sitting quietly in the waiting room his pulse was 88. He complains very much of <u>dizziness,</u> so much so that he is very <u>uncertain in his movements & actions.</u> The dizziness & weakness almost <u>incapacitate him from doing any work.</u> He is also (trinfld) with <u>muscular rheumatism</u> & has complained of this about all winter. He has had several attacks of acute nephritis, <u>high colored urine & scanty.</u> The <u>last sample of urine examined showed</u> **a trace of albumen.** With the muscular <u>rheumatism & the weak heart action he is practically incapacitated from performing manual labor.</u>

Frank R. Glaston

05-??-1901   (received 05-16-1901)
General law - PHYSICIAN'S AFFIDAVIT, State of New York, County of Erie, SS:
In the pension claim No. 2x,xxx: of Jacob Bowles, late of Co. K. 115th Reg't. Pa. Vol. Inf., Personally came before me, a Notary Public, in and for the aforesaid County and State Frank R. Glaston, a citizen of Buffalo NY, whose Post-Office address is 634 Michigan St., well known to me to be reputable and entitled to credit, and who, being duly sworn, declares in relation to the aforesaid case as follows:

That he is a Practicing Physician and that he has been acquainted with said soldier for over 4 years, and thatI have already made two affidavits in the claim of Mr. Bowles to which I invite the attention of the board. **From the history of the case I learn that** <u>he had been injured by a shot & that he has been more or less incapacitated from performing his usual vocation since then.</u> Furthermore **I learn that** <u>he has</u> <u>contracted rheumatism while in service & that he has been troubled since then. The exposure while in service would account for the muscular rheumatism as it would also account for the condition of the heart & kidneys already referred to in a previous communication. The condition of his heart is such that one would not expect to find it to be caused by old age alone & since</u>

he has been troubled with it ever since his service in the Army it is only reasonable that the service was responsible for it.

Frank R. Glaston

05-14-1901

General law.   GENERAL AFFIDAVIT

State of New York, County of Erie, SS: In the matter of claim for original invalid pension No. 2x,xxx of Jacob Bowles, Co. K. 115th Regt. Pa. Vol. Inf.

On this 14" day of May, A.D. 1901, personally appeared before me, a Notary Public in and for the aforesaid County, duly authorized to administer oaths, Jacob Bowles, aged 60 years, a resident of Buffalo, in the County of Erie and State of New York, whose Post-office address is 27 Spruce St, Buffalo, NY., well known to me to be reputable and entitled to credit, and who, being duly sworn, declares in relation to the aforesaid case as follows:

I am the claimant above named. About the last week of April, 1862, while at Yorktown Va. I began to suffer from rheumatism, attended with aches & pains all over me. This no doubt was caused from exposures for we were greatly exposed at this time. This rheumatism was principally in the muscles, but at times in my joints when it first came on it appeared in my left knee. During all of the remainder of my service, I suffered more or less from said rheumatism. I have suffered from disease of heart since I received a shock at the battle of Fair Oaks Va. in service of 1862. Also, since that time I have suffered from a lame back across my kidneys, and up & down the spinal column. It is a fact that I have been greatly broken down in health since I contracted said diseases & disabilities while in the service, aforesaid.   Jacob Bowles

06-07-1901 Atty P. date & cause of rej. & ev. since filed not suf. to warrant change of action.

Well, after all that, it's still no use. Even including two personal physicians and two contemporary witnesses is not enough to convince the board that his injuries are service-related.

06-15-1901
Declaration for Invalid Pension.
Act of June 27, 1890 and May 9, 1900.
State of New York, County of Erie, SS: On this 15th day of June A.D. one thousand nine hundred and one personally appeared before me, a Notary Public within and for the County and State aforesaid, <u>Jacob Bowles, aged 60 years</u>, a resident of the city of Buffalo, County of Erie, State of New York, who, being duly sworn according to law, declares that he is the identified Jacob Bowles who was enrolled on the 18 day of February 1862 in Co. K 115th Regt. Pa. vol. Inf. in the service of the United States in the war of the rebellion, and served at least ninety days and <u>was honorably discharged at Philladelphia Pa. on the 1" day of May 1863. That he is Partially unable to earn a support by manual labor by reason of Rheumatism, disease of heart and kidneys, affection of back, catarh of head and throat, and general debility</u>.

He **requests** an <u>early Medical examination</u> to determine his right to said pension.

That said <u>disabilities,</u> are not due to vicious habits, and are, to the best of his knowledge and belief, of a <u>permanent character</u>. That he has applied for pension under application No. 2x,xxx – gen law.
ATT'Y FILED
That he has not been employed in the military or naval service otherwise than as stated above. That he makes this declaration for the purposes of being placed on the pension roll of the United States, under the provision of the Act of June 27, 1890 and May 9,1900. He hereby appoints Willard H. Peck, of Buffalo, N.Y., his true and lawful attorney, to prosecute his claim, and he directs that the sum of Ten Dollars be paid to said Attorney.

That his post-office address is 27 Spruce St. Buffalo, County of Erie, State of New York.

(1)   Cameron Groat
        X   Jacob Bowles
(2)   Thomas Hobson
        Signature of Claimant The witnesses who write sign here

06-24-1901   Buffalo, N.Y. Atty Peck advised marriage cir. sent. J.S.W.

Primary for Jacob Bowles is to secure a pension. But the board now demands a new kind of submission. At about this time the Bureau of Pensions appears to become interested in some of the more mundane details of the veterans under its authority. Apparently, it is time to firm up the stature of its record-keeping. We might have ignored this at the present time, but, interestingly, this information begins to wriggle its way into other aspects of Jacob Bowles life, which take on larger and larger character as his struggles for a pension decrease.

First Marriage Circular

I guess that by June of 1901 things have settled enough at the Bureau of Pensions for them to focus more and more on record-keeping. This is to the benefit of all ex-soldiers. Tracking their families through marriage, children and location will become a very important part of the function that the Bureau of Pensions plays. Jacob Bowles also has the opportunity to add to this record base.

06-27-1901   Department of the Interior, Bureau of Pensions, Washington D.C., June 24, 1901

Marriage Circular

Mid Div., GSW Ex'r, O.S. No 21,627, Jacob Bowles, Co K, 115 Reg't Pa-Inf

Sirs:

Will you kindly answer, at your earliest convenience, the questions enumerated below? The information is requested for future use, and it may be of great value to your family. Very respectfully, H. Chuy Sounds

Mr. Jacob Bowles, Buffalo, NY

No 1. Are you a married man? If so, please state your wife's full name, and her maiden name. Answer: <u>Yes. I married a Widdow Mrs. Elizebeth Otis.</u>

No 2. When, where, and by whom were you married? Answer: by the <u>Rev Percy W. Smith Rector of Fort Erie Ont.</u>

No 3. What record of marriage exists? Answer: first and second. <u>My first marriage was in 1860 – 20th of August, Previn Town, Westmoreland Co, Pa.</u>

No 4. Were you previously married? If so, please state the name of your former wife and the date and place of her death. Answer: <u>name of first Addaline Pa..th.... died ...14th, 1869 Allegheny</u> City, Pa. (partially illegible)

No 5. Have you any children living? If so, please state their names and the dates of their birth. Answer: <u>Have three sons living by my first wfe –</u>

     <u>Daniel M. was born February 12 1864</u>
     <u>Jared B. was born November 20 1865</u>
     <u>Frank C. was born April 28 1868</u>
     <u>have a step daughter Mrs. Ellie Glaston was born April 16 1874</u>

Date of reply, June 27, 1901
     Jacob Bowles

06-27-1901
MARRIAGE CERTIFICATE. <u>Diocese of Niagara – On the 27<u>th</u> day of June 1901 Were Married Jacob F. Bowles of the City of Buffalo N.Y. (Widower) and Elizabeth Oties of the City of Buffalo (Widow) by me, Percy W. Smith, Rector of St. Paul's Church, Fort Erie, Ont.</u> This Marriage was solemnized between us.　　　　　Jacob F. Bowles, Elizabeth Oties Witnesses: E. Smith, P.A. Smith
<u>I Certify that the above particulars are truly extracted from the Register of Marriages kept in St. Paul's Rectory, Fort Erie, this 29<u>th</u> day of July 1918</u>. D. Russell Smith, Rector of St. Paul's Church, Fort Erie, Ont.

     The Reverend D. Russell Smith certifies to me that this is a true and correct transcript taken from the Marriage Records of St. Paul's Church now in his keeping as Pastor. The Church has no official seal. John J. Callahan, Notary Public.
- Certificate on file in Pension Office.

     And then back to the battle for the pension! An evidently older man now – Jacob's hair is no longer dark, but now either gray or white!

07-03-1901
SURGEON'S CERTIFICATE
Original Pension Claim No. 2x,xxx
Jacob Bowles, Company K Reg't 115 Pa. Inf., 27 Spruce St.,
Buffalo, N.Y.
Address of Board – <u>Buffalo</u>, New York;   July 3, 1901
Cause of Disability: <u>(1) Rheumatism, (2) Dis. heart. (3)</u>
<u>Kidneys. (4) Affection of back. (5) Catarrh of head. (6) General</u>
<u>debility</u>.

    Birthplace, Pennsylvania. Age 60 years; height 5.8;
weight 162 pounds; complexion Dark; color of eyes Brown;
    <u>color of hair Gray</u>; occupation Contractor; permanent
marks and scars other than those described below, -----------.

    We hereby certify that upon examination we find the
following objective conditions:

Pulse rate   sitting 84,   standing 87,   after exercise 84
Respiration   sitting 21,   standing 22,   after exercise 30,
                          temperature 98.5

    He receives a pension of xxxxxxxxx dollars per month.
He makes the following statement in regard to the origin of his
disabilities and date when first discovered by him: (1.)
<u>Rheumatism. Has aches and pains in the muscles of his arms and</u>
<u>legs which has troubled him for 25 years or more – worse in</u>
<u>inclement weather</u>.

    (2.) <u>Disease of heart.</u> Has <u>palpitation, fluttering</u> and
<u>shortness of breath</u> upon brisk exercise, <u>began to suffer from this</u>
<u>condition at the battle of Fair Oaks, May 31, 1862, and it has</u>
<u>lasted him until the present time.</u>

    (3.) <u>Disease of kidneys. Has had pain in his back over</u>
<u>the region of the kidneys ever since the war; it hurts him to stoop</u>
<u>or lift.</u>

    (4.) <u>Affection of back.</u> He has described this condition
in the foregoing count.

    (5.) <u>Catarrh of head and throat.</u> About 12 years ago he
began to have difficulty in breathing through his nose and throat
irritation – a condition that has annoyed him from that time until

now; he has employed several nose and throat doctors without complete relief.

(6.) General debility. For several years past – 5 or 6 – has been unable to do any hard work on account of weakness

(1-2) Rheumatism – Disease of heart. All joints, muscles and tendons are free from swelling or enlargement, tenderness or stiffness, atrophy or contraction, and there is no limitation of motion. Back's curves and curvatures are normal and there are no ciatrices or evidence of injury to the spinal column or any tissues of the back. The heart's apex impulse is normally located as evidenced by inspection and palpation; the area of cardiac dulness is not increased; there are no murmurs, dilatation, hypertrophy, dyspnea, edema or cyanosis.

(3.) Disease of kidneys. Urinary specimen 2 oz.; color bright yellow; specific gravity 1015; reaction acid; no albumin; no sugar; no edema or other evidence of disease of the kidneys.

(5.) Catarrh of head and throat. Nose: right – there is a small spur from the base of the septum; left side, the septum is slightly deviated to the left constricting air space. Throat: Shows general congestion of the fauses with chronic follicular pharyngitis; tubes perfious; he hears ordinary voice at 6 ft. in both ears. (both drumheads are thickened and somewhat retracted).

(6.) General debility. He is not anemic; color is good; skin is healthful; nutrition reasonably well conducted; palms are callused; indeed, **he is not suffering from general debility**.

Additional. He has an L-shaped cicatrix upon the right lower maxillar jaw; near and over the margin of the mental

William Thomas Potter – Pres., L. Burrows Jr. – Sec'y, J.G. Thompson – Treas.

(foramen); it is deeply attached to bone; all his teeth from the lower jaw are gone; this he claims is the result of an ulcerated tooth.

Note. While he has several disabilities, **yet none interfere** with the performance of manual labor as contemplated in the amendment of May 9, 1900. Hence we make no rating in the case.

Lungs. There are no rales or other indications of disease of the lungs as determined by inspection, palpation, auscultation and percussion; measurements of chest

at rest 34; full inspiration 36; full expiration 33.

No other disability claimed or found, and no evidence of vicious habits discovered.

William Thomas Potter – Pres., L. Burrows Jr. – Sec'y, J.G. Thompson – Treas.

Obviously, there is absolutely nothing wrong with this man!

1901

.....Eggars, Ex'r, No. 2xxxx, Act of June 27, 1890
Jacob F. Bowles, P.O. 27 Spruce St., Buffalo, Erie Co., N.Y.
Service K. 115th Pa. Inf   (9/26/19 M.O.R.)
Enlisted: Feb 18", 1862.   Discharged: May 1", 1863.

Application filed: June 17", 1901

Alleges: **REJECTED**
Any other Claim filed: 2x,xxx
Attorney: W.H. Peck, P.O. Buffalo, NY
Room 9, William Block

10-10-1901
O.I. Rejected, Act of June 27, 1890. INVALID PENSION O.I. No. 2x,xxx
Claimant Jacob Bowles, P.O. 27 Spruce St., Buffalo, New York
Rank Private, Company K, Regiment 115-Pa Vol Inf
Rate $-----per month, commencing June 17, 1901
REJECTED OCT 10 1901
Recognized Attorney W.H. Peck, P.O. Buffalo, N.Y.
Fee $10., Agent to pay.
APPROVALS:

<u>Submitted for Rejection</u> Aug 27, 1901   Wiggins J.S.
        Examiner
Approved for Rheumatism, disease of heart, kidneys and back, catarrh of head and throat and general debility.
Approved for Rejection, not ratably disabled under the Act of June 27, 1890.
Sept 13, 1901 C.E.Rindrell, Legal Reviewer
        Clarke, Medical Examiner
        HC, Medical Reviewer
Sept 25", 1901 A.A. Aspinwall, Re-Reviewer
Sept 26, 1901 J.F. Rank,   Medical Referee   J.S.W.
Not pensioned under other laws.
Enlisted Feb. 17", 1862, and honorably discharged May 1", 1863.
Declaration filed June 17", 1901, alleges permanent disability, not due to vicious habits, from rheumatism, disease of heart and kidneys, affection of back, catarrh of head and throat and general debility.
No, M.C.   Claimant does write.

10-10-1901
Clmnt & Atty Peck infd of N.Y. Rej. C.R.

10-12-1901
Declaration for Invalid Pension.
Act of June 27, 1890 and May 9, 1900.
State of New York, County of Erie, SS: On this 12th day of June A.D. one thousand nine hundred and one personally appeared before me, a Notary Public within and for the County and State aforesaid, <u>Jacob Bowles, aged 60 years</u>, a resident of the city of Buffalo, County of Erie, State of New York, who, being duly sworn according to law, declares that he is the identified Jacob Bowles who was enrolled on the 18 day of February 1862 in Co. K 115th Regt. Pa. Vol. Inf. in the service of the United States in the war of the rebellion, and served at least ninety days and was honorably discharged at Philla. Pa. on the 1" day of May 1863.

That he is **wholly unable** to earn a support by manual labor by reason of Rheumatism, disease of heart and kidneys, affection of back, catarh of head and throat, and general debility.

That, as he was last examined before the medical board in Buffalo, N.Y. he respectfully requests an early examination before the board in **Springville**, Erie Co., N.Y.

That he respectfully **enters an earnest protest** against the recent advisory decision in his claim, for he has submitted the best of medical evidence in his claim under the general law to which he invites the attention.

That said disabilities, are not due to vicious habits, and are, to the best of his knowledge and belief, of a permanent character. That he has applied for pension under application No. 2x,xxx under both the general law and Act of June 27-1890. That he has never been employed in the military or naval service otherwise than as stated above. That he makes this declaration for the purposes of being placed on the pension roll of the United States, under the provision of the Act of June 27, 1890 and May 9-1900. He hereby appoints Willard H. Peck, of Buffalo, N.Y., his true and lawful attorney, to prosecute his claim, and he directs that the sum of Ten Dollars be paid to said Attorney. That his post-office address is 27 Spruce St. Buffalo, County of Erie, State of New York.

(1)   Charles H. Goodrell   X
          Jacob Bowles
(2)   John Hiteroft
          Signature of Claimant
                The witnesses who write sign here

10-21-1901
Hon. Wm. H. Ryan advised as to date & cause of rejection.
    J.S.W.

11-01-1901
Clmt order Ex. Bd. Springville N.Y. and Atty Peck and Hon. Wm. H. Ryan so advised.   J.S.W.

He requests another examination by the board. Probably in an effort to completely shut him up, the board agrees to submit him to an examination at Springville, New York. Will this elicit the great benefit he has been seeking? Or is it just another opportunity for defeat?

Partial Success at Springville

Since 1886 Jacob Bowles has ben relying more and more on the possibility that his salvation will come through finding the right medical board of examiners and the potential results of that exam. Jacob <u>knows</u> that he is disabled; he <u>knows</u> it is a direct result of what happened to him in the War. He is convinced that somehow, at some time, the examiners will put aside their prejudice and find him as deserving of a pension as he knows he is. Now, near the end of 1901, at the age of 61, he has another chance.

11-06-1901
SURGEON'S CERTIFICATE
Original Pension Claim No. 2x,xxx
Jacob Bowles, Company K Reg't 115 Pa. Inf., 27 Spruce St., Buffalo, N.Y.
Address of Board: **Springville**, N.Y. <u>Nov. 6th, 1901</u>
<u>Cause of Disability</u>: Rheumatism, disease of heart and kidneys, affection of back, catarrh of head and throat and general debility.

Birthplace, Penn. <u>Age 61 years;</u> height 5-7; weight 161 pounds; complexion fair; color of eyes hazel; color of hair black gray; occupation <u>Contract painter</u>; permanent marks and scars other than those described below, none.

We hereby certify that upon examination we find the following objective conditions:

Pulse rate	sitting 80,	standing 88,	<u>after exercise 119</u>
Respiration	sitting 19,	standing 21,	<u>after exercise 27,</u>
		temperature 98.8	

He receives a pension of no dollars per month. He makes the following statement in regard to the origin of his disabilities and date when first discovered by him: <u>My rheumatism first began to trouble me while I was in the service, have it in my</u>

arms and legs. I was stunned at the battle of Fair Oaks, and my heart has bothered me ever since. I have pain in my back at times, which I think is due to trouble with my kidneys, troubled since battle of Fair Oaks. I have had catarrh for about twelve years.

Erect, fairly well nourished, hands show no manual labor.

Rheumatism: - He alleges that the right arm is painful on motion, and there is slight crepitation in shoulders. There is tenderness in course of right sciatic nerve, and he alleges that the left bothers him in the same way at times. No structural changes, no other joints affected.

Heart:- Apex in 5th, space ¾ in. to right of nipple, evident to palpation, area of dulness, 2 ½ x 2 ½ inches, force fair regular no murmurs, no cyanosis edema or dyspnoea.

Ch.M.34 ½ - 38 – 37 ½ vesicular and percussion resonance normal.

There is a scar on the outer and posterior portion of left thigh 4 in. below upper portion of trochanter major, ¾ x 2 ½ inches. Depressed and tender not adherent. There is another scar on the posterior aspect of same leg, on the same plane, 2 ½ x 4 inches, depressed to the depth of one inch, adherent to subjacent tissues and tender. He alleges this is the result of a bruise at the battle of Fair Oaks.

Affection of back:- He alleges pain in the region of the kidneys, but there are no objective symptoms.

Catarrh of head and throat: The anterior nares are red and inflamed and covered with crusts, the pharynx is also inflamed, tonsils slightly involved, tubes pervious no deafness.

There is an irregular scar on the right lower portion of chin near the mental foramen one inch in diameter caused by a diseased tooth and inferior maxillary bone, the scar is depressed and slightly tender. Urine amber, acid, sp. gr. 1014, no sugar, no albumen.

No other disability found. We find that the aggregate permanent disability for earning a support by manual labor is due to contusion of thigh, sciatica and catarrh and <u>warrants a rate of six dollars</u>.

Wm. H. Jackson – Pres., W.A. McFarlane – Sec'y,
O.C. Strong – Treas.

01-21-1902
Clmt & W.H.Peck as to Rej. J.M.D.
O.I. <u>Rejected,</u> Act of June 27, 1890.
INVALID PENSION O.I. No. 2x,xxx
Claimant Jacob Bowles, P.O. 27 Spruce St., Buffalo, New York
Rank Private, Company K, Regiment 115-Pa Vol Inf
Rate $-----per month, commencing October 14, 1901
<u>REJECTED</u> Jany 21, 1902
Recognized Attorney Willard H. Peck, P.O. Buffalo, N.Y.
Fee $10., Agent to pay.
APPROVALS:
Submitted for Adm Dec 3",1901   Wiggins J.S.   Examiner
<u>Approved for Rheumatism, disease of heart and kidneys, affection of back, catarrh of head and throat and general debility. Former rejection referred to Med. Ref. under Act of March 6, 1896.</u>
Jan. 3, 1902   Wm. Hatton, Legal Reviewer
Jany 9, 1902   A.B. Sniggett, Re-Reviewer
Approved for Rejection, <u>A ratable degree of disability is not shown</u> under Act of June 27, 1890.
          Brandt, Medical Examiner   Cooke, Medical Reviewer
          Jan 14, 1902   J.F. Rank, Medical Referee   S.J.E.
Not pensioned under other laws.
Enlisted Feb. 17", 1862, and honorably discharged May 1", 1863.
Declaration filed June 17", 1901, alleges permanent disability, not due to vicious habits, from rheumatism, disease of heart and kidneys, affection of back, catarrh of head and throat and general debility.

Oct 14-1901. Alleged rheumatism, disease of heart and kidneys, affection of back, catarrh of head and throat, and general debility.

Hon. Wm. H. Ryan, M.C.   Claimant does write.

02-02-1902

Hon. D.S. Alexander date & cause of <u>rejection</u>.   J.S.W.

I think there are probably few statements more ironic than "Approved for Rejection." But owing to the nature of these pre-printed government forms, this is often the result. There is a line titled "Approved for." So then the examiner fills out the form, entering the word "REJECTION." Hence, you are approved. You are approved, for Rejection.

Now this last interaction with the board is a little bit hard to follow. The doctors at Springville have granted him $6.00 of pensionability. But the board still rejects his request. He has the board of doctors willing to grant him a pension based on his condition, but it's not enough to get the other authorities to designate the pension as a condition of injury during the war.

In February of 1902, Jacob Bowles specifically addresses this anomaly.

02-08-1902

SUPPLEMENTAL DECLARATION FOR INVALID PENSION – Act of June 27, 1890

State of New York, County of Erie, SS:

On this 8th day of February, A.D. one thousand nine hundred & two personally appeared before me, a Notary Public within and for the County and State aforesaid, <u>Jacob Bowles, aged 61</u> years, a resident of the City of Buffalo, County of Erie, State of New York, who, being duly sworn according to law, declares that he is the identical Jacob Bowles who was enrolled on the 18th day of February, 1862 in Co. K. 115th Regt. Pa. Vols. Inft. in the service of the United States in the war of the rebellion, and served at least ninety days and was <u>honorably</u>

discharged at Philladelphia Pa. on the 1st day of May, 1863. That he was disabled for earning a support by manual labor in a pensionable degree on 21 of June, 1901, the date of filing his original declaration, by reason of the following disabilities: Rheumatism, disease of heart and kidneys, affection of back, catarrh of head & throat & general debility. That he is also disabled for earning a support by the above named disabilities. Claimant believes that the medical board at Buffalo N.Y. & Springville N.Y. **did** rate him in a Pensionable degree, also Claimant wishes to draw the Pension Bureau's attention to the Medical affidavit of Cecil A. Keller M.D. & Frank R. Glaston M.D. as evident to the same – **unable to do manual labor**.

The said disabilities are not due to vicious habits, and are, to the best of his knowledge and belief, of a permanent character, and that he is now entirely disabled for earning a support by manual labor in consequence of same. That he has applied for pension No. 2x,xxx under General Law, & Act June 27/90 & May 9/00. That he is not a pensioner under Certificate No. ------- ---- under ------.

That he is a claimant for pension under other laws. That he has not been employed in the military or naval service of the United States prior to February 18th, 1862, or subsequent to May 1st, 1863.

That he makes this declaration for the purpose of **reopening his claim** and being placed on the pension-roll of the United States, under the provisions of the Act of June 27, 1890 & May 9, 1900. He also requests that his original or first claim filed under the said Act, be re-examined and considered under the provisions of the Act approved March 6, 1896, and also under the decision of the Hon. Assistant Secretary of the Interior, of June 17, 1896, in the case of James J. Burkee, Vol. 8. P. D., p. 152, giving construction to said Act, and that he be given an opportunity to show by evidence that his claim, if allowed, should date back to the time of filing his original or first application for pension under the Act of June 27, 1890. He hereby appoints, with full power of substitution and revocation,

Willard H. Peck of Buffalo, County of Erie, State of New York, his true and lawful attorney, to prosecute this claim, and he directs that the sum of Ten Dollars be paid to said attorney.
That his post office address is #27 Spruce St., Buffalo, County of Erie, State of New York.
Attest: John Fliteroft
Claimant's signature   Jacob Bowles
           Charles H. Gosdrell
                    Two witnesses who can write sign here

03-01-1902
Atty Peck for Med. tes showing dis. & degree of your before order.   J.S.W.

08-14-1902
PHYSICIAN'S AFFIDAVIT, washed-out and unreadable;
Received @ US Pension Office, Aug 14, 1902.

09-10-1902
Clmt Order Cp Lockport N.Y. & Atty Peck advised – J.S.W.

1902 – Lockport Comes Through!

Another exam, another throw of the dice, another attempt to convince someone of his real situation. Months and years pass. The process is tedious, but Jacob Bowles is determined that his truth will out. His truth: the Pension Board's fiction. The Board's truth: his fiction. Are they all living in two different worlds? How can it be that every time they test him, they find a different person than the one he knows he is? Daily, he suffers his disability. He endures it; he experiences the fullness of it. And then they confront him: you have a bit of a problem, probably of your own making. Go away.

10-01-1902
SURGEON'S CERTIFICATE
Act June 27" 1890. Amended by Act May 9" 1900.
Original Pension Claim No. 2xxxx.
Jacob Bowles, Company K., Reg't 115th Pa. Infnt
27" Spruce St., Buffalo, NY
Address of Board: **Lockport**, New York   October 1", 1902
Rheumatism, Disease of Heart and Kidneys, affection of back, Catarrh of Head & Throat and General Debility.
He receives a pension of No dollars per month. He makes the following statement in regard to the origin of his disabilities and date when first discovered by him: He has had rheumatism since 1863. Short breath and heart disease for 18 years. Trouble in back and kidneys since Battle of Fair Oaks May 31st, 1862. Catarrh of head and throat for 12 years. Unable to do full days work since service.
       The outline of the human skeleton and figure upon the back of this certificate should be used to indicate precisely the

location of a disease or injury, the entrance and exit of a missile, an amputation, etc.

Birthplace Allegheny Pa.; age 61 years; height 5# 8 in.; weight 170 pounds; complexion Dark; color of eyes Hazel, color of hair Grey; occupation Contractor; permanent marks and scars other than those described below, No.

We hereby certify that upon examination we find the following objective conditions:

Pulse rate   sitting, 80   standing 88   after exercise 110
Respiration   sitting, 19   standing, 22   after exercise, 27
                        temperature 98 6/10.

Rheumatism --- Crepitation and tenderness in both shoulder joints, limitation of action by pain only. Also tenderness in both lumbar regions thighs, hips, and in both knees. Stoops to floor with difficulty.

Measure Ac- ax right, 18 ½, left 19 inches, biceps flexed Right 12, left 11 ½, buttocks 19 ½ alike, middle thighs 18 alike, above knee right 14. left 13 ½. over knees right 14, left 13 1/2 . below knees, right 12 ½, left 12. Calf 14 alike, ankles 8 ½ alike.

Heart. --- apex beat in 5th interspace ½ inch inside nipple line, area from 2nd to 5th interspace on 3rd rib, 3 ½ on 4th, 4 on 5th rib, 3 ½ inches from centre of sternum. A murmur with and following 2nd sound at upper base transmitted down sternum, action is feeble, rapid rhythm, disturbed. Hypertrophy and dilatation. Dyspnoea on exercise. No cyanosis or edema.

Catarrh --- a Uvula long. tonsils ragged. crusts in case. Eustachii permable.

URINE. Sp. gr. 1010, Pale. acid. No sugar or albumen. His hands show no evidence of manual labor. **All muscles are soft and flaby and muscles are tender**. Although he weighs 170 pounds he is now **anaemic**.

We find the aggregate permanent disability for earning a support by manual labor is due to Rheumatism, Disease of heart, Catarrh, and Debility and not due to vicious habits, and warrants a rate of $8.00.

A. Williame, Pres.   W.Q.Huggins, Sec'y   W.L. Dupert, Treas.

11-25-1902

Medical Division – Bureau of Pensions, Washington D.C.   Nov 25, 1902

No. Claim 2x,xxx, Claimant Jacob Bowles,

Soldier Jacob Bowles, Co. K, 115 Reg't Pa. Vol.

Respectfully returned to Chief – Board of Review.

A disability from rheumatism disease of heart and nose – pharyngeal catarrh ratable at $8. under Act of June 27-1890; is shown in this claim. No other disability affecting rate.

        Brandt, Medical Examiner

        Approved: Sam Houston, Medical Referee

12-05-1902

105xxxx Buffalo, Act of June 27, 1890.

INVALID PENSION O.I. No. 2x,xxx

Claimant Jacob Bowles, P.O. 27 Spruce St., Buffalo, New York

Rank Private, Company K, Regiment 115-Pa Vol Inf

Rate $8 per month, **commencing February 12, 1902**

Pensioned for partial inability to earn a support by manual labor.

Recognized Attorney Willard H. Peck, P.O. Buffalo, N.Y.

Fee $10., Agent to pay.

APPROVALS:

Submitted for Adm Nov. 17",1902

        Wiggins J.S.   Examiner

Approved for Rheumatism, disease of heart and naso-pharyngeal catarrh. Rej affection of back, kidney trouble & genl. debility.

No dis subj appr N.A. claim under act March 6, 96 to M.R.

Evidence filed.

Nov. 28, 1902 L. A. Branddury, Legal Reviewer

Dec 2, 1902   E. Singletary, Re-Reviewer

Approved for rheumatism, disease of heart and naso pharyngeal catarrh

Aggregate of disabilities shown, permanent in character, $8.00

Former rejections adhered to

Byington, Medical Examiner   Cooke, Medical Reviewer

Dec 5, 1902   Sam Houston, Medical Referee
Not pensioned under other laws.
Enlisted Feb. 17", 1862, and honorably discharged May 1",
1863.
Declaration filed Feb 12", 1902, alleges permanent disability, not
due to vicious habits, from rheumatism, disease of heart and
kidneys, affection of back, catarrh of head and throat and general
debility. Also claims benefit of Act of March 6-1896.
     No, M.C.   Claimant does write.

12-13-1902
Act of June 27, 1890
Invalid Series ----------   Cert. No. 105xxxx
Name, Jacob Bowles; Rank, Priv
Service Co K 115th Pa Vol Inf
Agency – Original Roll: ~~Buffalo~~
Transf'd   ------- to Gr 1
1" Issue, Class Orig'l, Fee $10
Issued Dec 8, 1902.   Mailed Dec 13, 1902
Rate and Period, $8, from Feb 12, 1902
Partial inability to earn a support by manual labor.

*The universe reels! Truth and fiction have contrived to
cross paths here. Somehow, the Lockport board has flown under
the radar. I can see no change in any of the details that would
have gained Jacob Bowles his pension payment, except maybe
that the men involved in the final review may be different than
those who went before. The diagnosis outlined above, if it had
come from any previous board would have resulted in exactly the
same outcome: disabled, but not due to the war. But, somehow,
he is now approved for disability. Dig through this document,
and declare to me what is the essential difference that results in
a pension? Can you do it? I cannot. BUT! The door is finally
open. And Jacob Bowles is not slow to request more.*

01-17-1903

APPLICATION FOR <u>RECONSIDERATION AND ARREARS</u>
– Act of June 27, 1890

Under the Provisions of the Act of March 6, 1896

State of New York, County of Erie, SS: On this 17" day of Jan,
A.D. one thousand nine hundred and three, personally appeared
before me, Jacob Bowles, a Comr of Deeds within and for the
County and State aforesaid <u>Jacob Bowles, aged 62 </u>years, a
resident of the City of Buffalo, County of Erie, State of New
York who, being duly sworn according to law, declares that he is
a pensioner of the United States enrolled at the Buffalo N.Y.
Pension Agency at the rate of Eight (8) dollars per month under
Certificate No. 1,05x,xxx by reason of disabilities from Partial
mobility to earn a support by manual labor. that his Military
service was as follows: Private in Co K. 115th Pa Vols Infty.
That he was disabled from earning a support by manual labor in
a pensionable degree on the 12" day of October 1901, the date of
making original application under the Act of June 27, 1890, by
reason of <u>the following disabilities: Rheumatism & disease of
heart. 2 Kidneys affecting of back. Catarrh of head & throat &
general debility, and was rated six dollars per month under said
application before the board at Springville N.Y. Nov 6/01.</u>
That the disabilities alleged in his said original application under
the Act of June 27, 1890, <u>existed in a pensionable degree at the
date of the filing</u> of his said <u>original application</u>. That he makes
this application for the purpose of <u>having his original application
reconsidered and his pension made to date from the filing of said
original application, viz: on the 14 or 15 day of October, 1901 in
accordance with the provisions of the Act of March 6, 1896.</u>

      He hereby appoints, with full power of substitution and
revocation,   Willard H. Peck of Buffalo N.Y. his true and
lawful attorney to prosecute his claim, the fee to be Ten Dollars.
That his Post-Office address is #27 Spruce St, Buffalo, County of
Erie, State of New York. Jacob Bowles   John J. McCaffrey
    (Claimant's Signature)   William J. Wilson
              (Two witnesses who write sign here.)

04-11-1903

DECLARATION FOR INCREASE OF PENSION – Under the Acts of June 27, 1890 and May 9, 1900.

State of New York, County of Erie, SS: On this 11" day of April A.D. nineteen hundred and three personally appeared before me, a Commr of Deeds within and for the County and State aforesaid, <u>Jacob Bowle aged 62 years,</u> late a member of Co K. 115 Regiment, Pa Vols Inft. a resident of the City of Buffalo, County of Erie, State of New York, who, being duly sworn according to law, declares that he is a pensioner of the United States under the Act of June 27, 1890, enrolled at the Buffalo N.Y. Pension Agency, at the rate of Eight (8) dollars per month, by reason of <u>partial inability</u> to earn a support by manual labor, his Pension Certificate being numbered 1,05x,xxx. That he believes himself to <u>be entitled to an increase of pension on account of the disabilities heretofore allowed, namely Rheumatism and disease of heart & kidney, affecting of back, catarrh of head & throat and general debility, Causing inability to earn a support by manual labor</u>.

And **would request to go before the medical Board at Lockport or Springville** N.Y. for examination.

That he appoints, with full power of substitution and revocation, Willard H. Peck, of Buffalo, County of Erie, State of New York, his true and lawful Attorney, to prosecute his claim.

His post-office address is #27 Spruce St, Buffalo, County of Erie, State of New York.

Claimant's signature   Jacob Bowles

Attest: John Fliteroft
John J. McCaffrey
Two witnesses who can write sign here.

04-13-1903

DEPARTMENT OF THE INTERIOR, Bureau of Pensions, Washington D.C.   Apr 10, 1903

Record & Pension Office, War Department, Apr 11 1903, 225xxxx

Woodbury   East Div., G.F.W., Ex'r

Respectfully referred to the Chief of the Record and Pension Office, War Department, <u>requesting a full military and medical history of the soldier and his personal description and age at enlistment.</u>

2 enclosures

No other report on file,   Cert No. 105xxxx, Name Jacob Bowles, Co K, 115th Reg't Pa. Inf.

J.L.Davenport, Acting Commissioner

Record and Pension Office, War Department, Washington   Apr 11 1903

Respectfully returned to the Commissioner of Pensions, with the information that in the case of Jacob Bowles age 23 yrs, Co K. 115 Pa Inf the military records furnish nothing additional to former statement herewith <u>except roll Feb 28.62 shows him present same to April 30.62.</u> Name not found on rolls Feb 28 & Apr 30.63. For description see S.C.D. a duplicate of which was sent to P.D. May 19.63.

EAST DIV. APR 13 1903 RECEIVED

Medical records that have indexed (or discovered) since the statement of Apl 21/73, herewith returned, was made show the <u>following additional information: treated July 7 to August 17/62 (diagnosis not stated).</u> Nothing additional found.

U.S. Pension Office APR 11 1903

By Authority of the Secretary of WarF. C. Aninworth
     Chief, Record and Pension Office

Now that Jacob Bowles is approved for pension, the board makes a request for his full military and medical history (maybe they could have done this a long time ago?). Somehow, the pension board has managed to get its hands on more

information involving his apparent AWOL standing and some of his treatment in the hospital. And with the door opened, Jacob Bowles wastes no time. Now that he has been approved, he reaches back for what should have been approved years in the past. How far can he get this time?

04-14-1903
Under Act of June 27, 1890   (3-1639)
INCREASE
Claim to -----------, No. 1,05x,xxx
Jacob Bowles, P.O. #27 Spruce St, Buffalo, N.Y.
Application filed Jan 22, 1903
State Service, K-115 Pa Inf
APR 10 1903 A. 4. returned G.F.W.
APR 14 1903 Ex. Buffalo, Erie Co., N.Y.
Atty W H Peck   ntfd.   G.F.W.
Disability, --------------
Attorney, W.H. Peck, P.O. Buffalo, N.Y.
A.R.   J.H.

04-15-1903
Under Act of June 27, 1890   (3-1639)
INCREASE
Claim to -----------, No. 105xxxx
Jacob Bowles, P.O. 27. Spruce St, Buffalo, N.Y.
Application filed Apl 15, 1903
State Service, K-115 Pa Inf
Disability, --------------
Attorney, W.H. Peck, P.O. Buffalo, N.Y.
M.F.G.

04-22-1903
SURGEON'S CERTIFICATE
Increase Pension Claim No. 1,05x,xxx
Jacob Bowles, Company K., Reg't 115 Pa.. Inf.
27 Spruce St., Buffalo, N.Y.

Address of Board: **Buffalo**, New York   April 22, 1903
(1) Rheumatism. (2) Dis.Heart. (3) Naso-pharyngeal catarrh. (4) Affection of back. (5) Kidney trouble. (6) General debility.
He receives a pension of Eight dollars per month. He makes the following statement in regard to the origin of his disabilities and date when first discovered by him:

(1.) Rheumatism. For the past 25 years has been troubled at intervals with aches and pains in his right and left leg; these locations seem to interchange the pain with each other, worse during wet weather.

(2.) Disease of heart. About 13 years past, more or less, has been troubled with palpitation and shortness of breath upon any excitement or active exercise.

(3.) Naso-pharyngeal catarrh. For the past 16 years has been under treatment for this disease, but does not know how long previous to that time it troubled him; has difficulty in breathing through his nose, with cough, expectoration and throat irritation.

(4.) Affection of back. Ever since his army service has been troubled more or less with pain in his back; it hurts him to stoop or lift.

(5.) Kidney trouble. Soon after his discharge from the service began to have pain in the back, together with distress and frequency of micturation.

(6.) General debility. For several years past has been unable to do any hard work on account of feebleness.

Additional. About 11 years ago had trouble with his teeth which resulted in disease of the jaw, for which he was operated upon.

Birthplace Pennsylvania; age 62 years; height 5.8; weight 168 pounds; complexion Dark; color of eyes Brown, color of hair Grey; occupation Painter; permanent marks and scars other than those described below, No.

We hereby certify that upon examination we find the following objective conditions:
Pulse rate   sitting, 78   standing 78   after exercise 81

Respiration   sitting, 18   standing, 18   after exercise, 20
temperature 98.3.

(1-2-4.) Rheumatism – Disease of heart – Affection of back. The muscles of both arms are tender to pressure; the right shoulder-joint crepitates upon passive motion; otherwise, all joints, muscles and tendons are free from swelling or enlargement, tenderness or stiffness, atrophy or contraction, and there is no limitation of motion. There are no swelling, cicatrices, atrophies, or other indication of disease of the back. The point and area of apex impulse is evident to inspection and palpation at the 5th interspace 1 in. inside the nipple line; the are of cardiac dulness is not increased; its rhythm is natural; there are no murmurs, neither is there dilatation, hypertrophy, dyspnea, edema or cyanosis.   Rating – 4/18

(3.) Naso-pharyngeal catarrh. Nose; right, the posterior parts of both turbinates are hypertrophied and in contact with the septum; left, the inferior turbinate is much hypertrophied. Throat: fauces congested; tubes pervious; he hears ordinary conversation at 6 ft. with either ear. Lungs: there are no rales or other indications of disease of the lungs as determined by inspection, palpation, ausculation and percussion; measurement of chest at rest 38; full inspiration 37; full expiration 34. Disability – Naso-pharyngeal catarrh.   Rating – 4/18

(5.) Disease of kidneys. Urinary specimen 2 oz.; color bright yellow; reaction acit; specific gravity 1014; no sugar; no albumin; no edema, or other evidence of disease of the geniot-urinary organs.

Rating – 0/0

William Thomas Potter, Pres. L. Burrows Jr., Sec'y
J.G.Thompson, Treas.

(6.) General Debility. His muscles are soft, but he is fairly well nourished and is not anemic.

Rating – 0/0

Additional. There is an irregular cicatrix upon the right lower jaw L-shaped, with the L placed horizontally; it extends 1 ¼ in. below the right angle of the mouth to the mental foramen, then downward losing itself in the submental tissue; it is attached and dragging; the bone is roughened and indicates loss of tissue; he gives a history of first a diseased tooth; then necrosis of the bone and finally, operation for the removal of necrosed bony tissue; he has no teeth remaining either above or below, though loss of teeth in the upper jaw began prior to the traumatism herein described; it causes a marked disfigurement and is a serious disability.

Rating – 6/18

No other disability claimed or found, and no evidence of vicious habits discovered.

William Thomas Potter, Pres. L. Burrows Jr.,
Sec'y   J.G.Thompson, Treas.

09-30-1903
Cert. No. 105xxxx – Act June 27, 1890
Increase   INVALID PENSION
Claimant Jacob Bowles, P.O. 27 Spruce St., Buffalo, Erie Co., New York
Rank Private, Company K, Regiment 115th Pa. Vol. Inf.
Rate ---- per month, commencing
Pensioned for ---------------   Sept 30th 1903 REJECTED
Recognized Attorney Willard H. Peck, P.O. Buffalo, N.Y.
Fee $2., Agent to pay.
APPROVALS:
Submitted for September 16, 1903
M. B. Saunders   Examiner
Approved for Rheumatism, disease of heart & naso-pharyngeal catarrh. (rej) and disease of kidneys & back and general debility. (new) alleged Jan'y 22, 1903.
Claim under Act mar. 6-96 disposed of in this action.

Theord Sargent, E. Dir.   Sept 17, 1903
Approved for rheumatism, disease of heart and naso pharyngeal catarrh
Aggregate of disabilities shown, permanent in character, $8.00
No increase.

J Morrison, Medical Examiner
Shirley, Medical Reviewer
Sept 21, 1903 Sam Houston, Medical Referee

Enlisted Feb. 17", 1862, and honorably discharged May 1", 1863.

Pensioned at $8 per month. Last paid to ---------------

Rheumatism, disease of heart and naso-pharyngeal catarrh.

Present Claim, Act of June 27, 1890

Declaration filed January 22, 1903, alleges rheumatism, disease of heart and kidneys and back, naso-pharyngeal catarrh and general debility – and claims re-issue per Act March 6-1896.

Declaration filed April 15" 1903 alleges same disabilities.

    Claimant does write.

    Certificate not filed.

        No, M.C.

10-02-1903

Act of June 27, 1890

Invalid Series ----------   Cert. No. 105xxxx

Name, Jacob Bowles; Rank, Priv

Service Co K 115th Pa Vol Inf

Agency – Original Roll: ~~Buffalo~~

Transf'd   ------- to Gr 1

INDORSEMENTS

Sept 30" 1903 Increase rejected

Oct 2   W.H. Peck   M.B.E.

10-02-1903

DECLARATION FOR INCREASE OF PENSION –

Under the Acts of June 27, 1890 and May 9, 1900.

State of New York, County of Erie, SS: On this 2" day of Oct A.D. nineteen hundred and three personally appeared before me, a Comr of Deeds within and for the County and State aforesaid, Jacob Bowles aged 62 years, late a member of Co K. 115 Regiment, Pa Vols Inft a resident of the City of Buffalo, County of Erie, State of New York, who, being duly sworn according to law, declares that he is a pensioner of the United States under the Act of June 27, 1890, enrolled at the Buffalo N.Y. Pension Agency, at the rate of Eight (8) dollars a month, by reason of partial inability to earn a support by manual labor, his Pension Certificate being numbered 105xxxx. That he believes himself to be entitled to an increase of pension on account of the disabilities heretofore allowed, namely Rheumatism and disease of heart & kidneys, lame back, catarrh of head & throat & general debility and said disabilities due cause inability to earn a support by manual labor and therefore justly entitled to the full rate under said Act. He has (hereto four) from same by physicians and **he cannot understand how the Bureau can take such actions.** He would request to be examined at **Lakeport or Batavia City**.

That he appoints, with full power of substitution and ervocation, Willard H. Peck, of Buffalo, County of Erie, State of New York, his true and lawful Attorney, to prosecute his claim.

His post-office address is 27 Spruce St, Buffalo, County of Erie, State of New York.

Claimant's signature   Jacob Bowles
Attest: John Fliteroft
Cameron Groat

Two witnesses who can write sign here.

Opposed for increases, but no decrease in his efforts now! Full speed ahead. Perhaps his attorney has encouraged him that the squeaky wheel gets the grease. Now it is apparent that he is not about to give up. After all, his disability started back when he was discharged. Somehow, he has to find the right board of physicians and the right bureaucrats to authorize all the necessary payments. And still, the years tick by. There is a sense of victory, but still a prevailing sense of unfairness.

02-15-1904
Under Act of June 27, 1890   (3-1639)
INCREASE
Cert. No. 1,05x,xxx
Jacob Bowles, P.O. #27 Spruce St, Buffalo, Erie Co., N.Y.
Application filed Oct 5, 1903 Service,   K.115- Pa. Inf-
~~Dec. 17/03   To Atty Peck for Med. Ex. for warrant exam~~
        W.P.M.
m Ex. Batavia, N.Y.   Feb 15-1904-Ord to Clmt Atty Peck
notified   M.W.
Attorney, W.H. Peck, P.O. Buffalo, N.Y.
M.W.   MdW

1904 – Jackpot at Batavia

Finally, after somehow releasing the floodwaters, Jacob gets more attention from the Examination Board of the Disability Bureau. It is almost as if the perception of the examiners is colored by the accumulated bulk of the past, rather than by present interpretation. As long as Jacob Bowles was not disabled enough to matter, and not disabled due to his service in the War, his disability should be ignored. Now that he has been found disabled, to whatever extent as a result of war injuries, his disability becomes a focus that must be pursued energetically.

03-02-1904
SURGEON'S CERTIFICATE
<u>Increase Pension Claim</u> No. 105xxxx
Jacob Bowles, Company K. 115 Reg't Pa.. Vol Inf.
27 Spruce St., Buffalo, N.Y.
Address of Board: **Batavia**, New York   Mch 2, 1904
Rheumatism dis. of heart & naso-pharyngeal catarrh & alleged dis. of kidneys, lower back & gen. debility-
He receives a pension of 8 dollars per month. He makes the following statement in regard to the origin of his disabilities and date when first discovered by him:
        <u>I am a painter by trade but have had to give it up so that now I only contract for jobs.</u>
        Birthplace Allegheny City, Pa.; <u>age 64 years</u>; height 5 ft 8; <u>weight 172 pounds</u>; <u>complexion florid</u>; color of eyes Brown, **color of hair White**; <u>occupation Painter</u>; permanent marks and scars other than those described below, None.
        We hereby certify that upon examination we find the following objective conditions:
Pulse rate   sitting, 76   standing 90   <u>after exercise 120</u>
Respiration   sitting, 14   standing, 18   <u>after exercise, 28</u>
                      temperature 98.5.

Rheumatism & Lower back – Claimant has rheumatism of right shoulder. Right shoulder measures 19 inches, Left 20. There is cupitus and motion of right shoulder is limited ¼. No other joints, tendons or muscles are affected.

Disease of Heart – Area of dulenum 2x2 inches. Apex beat is in 5th intercostal space evident to palpation. There are no (enelercarcliar minnnenenes). No dilitation or hypertrophy. No orcensn cyanosis or olys percorce.. Pulse 76.90.120 is irregular & weak. This is due to debility – not to organic disease.

Naso-catarrh – Claimant has severe naso-pharyngeal catarrh. Has ulcerations of the nasal septernis and a constant discharge running down the posterior naces. Both tonsils are hypertrophied & broken down. There is no deafness.

Disease of kidneys – Sp. Gr. 1012. Pale color. Acid reaction. Contains albumin in large (essanatates <quantities?>) 30%. Has chronic Bright's Disease.

General Debility – Claimant is weak & prematurely aged. & (nicicus). Has marked Areus Suriles & unable to do manual labor. This debility is due to Albuminism.

Right Inguenal hernia – Claimant has complete right inguenal hernia. Passes through the excoriated ring and descends into the scrotum. Tumor is 3 inches in diameter.

L. W. Skinner, Pres.   B. T. Thorness, Sec'y A. Prince, Treas. retainable by a trace

Scar in right jaw – There is a large 3 cornered scar made from an operation for necrosis of the jaw. No disability on account of it. We find that the aggregate permanent disability for earning a support by manual labor is due to Rheumatism, naso-pharyngeal catarrh, Bright's disease, general debility and right inguenal hernia is not due to vicious habits and warrants a rate of $12.

L. W. Skinner, Pres.   B. T. Thorness, Sec'y A. Prince, Treas.

Overnight, we see an incredible transformation! After countless years of being Superman, Jacob Bowles is finally revealed as an incredibly decrepit, worn down man.

What has happened here? Where did this come from? Suddenly, in March of 1904, myriad symptoms are discovered during the examination at Batavia that confirm the testimony of Jacob Bowles all the way back to his discharge from the service. Chronic Bright's Disease! What are some typical modern evaluations? Fatigue and Anorexia, Pain in the Head, Backache, abdominal pain, leg swelling, tachycardia, impaired kidney function. And yet every time he appeared for an exam, he seemed to be Superman. Who knows? What is the truth? It seems the doctors were always trying to do their best. And he had enough other complaints to mask the symptoms. But, the main point is that everything of which Jacob Bowles has been complaining is seen to be completely consistent. What will the pension board do now?

07-09-1904
M.M. 105xxxx   Buffalo
Cert. No. 105xxxx – Act June 27, 1890
Increase   INVALID PENSION
Claimant Jacob Bowles, P.O. 27 Spruce St., Buffalo, New York
Rank Private, Company K, Regiment 115, Pa. Vol. Inf
Rate $12- per month, commencing March 2, 1904
Pensioned for total inability to earn a support by manual labor.
Recognized Attorney W. H. Peck, P.O. Buffalo, N.Y.
Fee $2., Agent to pay.
APPROVALS:
Submitted for AD July 2, 1904   T. F. Monahan Examiner
Approved for Rheumatism, disease of heart & naso-pharyngeal catarrh. (Old) lame back, disease of kidneys, and general debility. (new) alleged Oct 5, 1903. Right-iningenal hernia
order 71
July 7, 1904   A.T.Siemmer, Legal Reviewer East Div.
Approved for rheumatism, disease of heart, kidneys, naso pharyngeal catarrh, right inguenal hernia and general debility.
Aggregate of disabilities shown, permanent in character, $12.
from March 2, 1904

Bullock, Medical Examiner   J. Lorno, Medical Reviewer
          July 9, 1904   Sam Houston, Medical Referee
Enlisted Feb. 17, 1862, and honorably discharged May 1, 1863.
Pensioned at $8 per month. Last paid to ---------------
Present Claim, Act of June 27, 1890
Declaration filed Oct 5, 1903, alleges increase and disease of
kidneys and back and general debility.
          Claimant does write.
          Certificate not filed.
                    No, M.C.

07-27-1904
Act of June 27, 1890
Invalid Series ----------   Cert. No. 105xxxx
Name, Jacob Bowles; Rank, Priv
Service Co K 115th Pa Vol Inf
Agency – Original Roll: ~~Buffalo~~
Transf'd   ------- to Gr 1
2" Issue, Class Inc, Fee $2
Issued July 14", 1904.   Mailed July 27, 1904
Rate and Period, $12, from Mar 2", 1904

1909 – An Act of Congress

Then, finally, we reach the year 1909. All of Jacob Bowles efforts have been spent. Now it has come down to the mercy of the United States government, chiefly the Houses of Congress. Finally, now, after his long and drawn out efforts to secure a pension, the government steps in and honors its soldiers. Finally, now, for the remaining years of his life, he will receive the maximum allowable pension.

01-28-1909
[PRIVATE – No. 93.] [H. R. 23850]
An Act Granting pensions and increase of pensions to certain soldiers and sailors of the civil war and certain widows and dependent relatives of such soldiers and sailors.
Be it enacted by the Senate and House of Representatives of the United States of America in Congress assembled, That the Secretary of the Interior be, and he is hereby, authorized and directed to place on the pension roll, subject to the provisions and limitations of the pension laws –
....
The name of Jacob Bowles, late of Company K, One hundred and fifteenth Regiment Pennsylvania Volunteer Infantry, and pay him a pension at the rate of **twenty-four dollars per month** in lieu of that he is now receiving.
....
Approved, January 28, 1909.

02-13-1909

Record Division, Department of the Interior, Bureau of Pensions

Claim No.   O.K.

J. C.

Certificate No. 105xxxx, Soldier Jacob Bowles, Service K 115 Pa Inf

Chief's Desk, Eastern Feb 13 1909

BY SPECIAL ACT Approved Jan 28, 1909

(3462)

G. C. Kniffin, Chief Division

02-16-1909

Special Act   Cert. No. 1,05x,xxx

Act June 27, 1890

P 105xxxx   Buffalo

Increase INVALID PENSION

Claimant Jacob Bowles, P.O. 27 Spruce Street, Buffalo, New York

Rank Private, Company K, Regiment 115 Pa Vol Inf

Rate $24- per month, commencing January 28, 1909

Pensioned under Special Act ~~inability to earn a support by manual labor~~.

Recognized Attorney

APPROVALS:

Submitted for Adm Feby 13, 1909

       M.A. Robinson   Examiner

Approved for Increase to $24 per month **under Special Act** approved January 28-1909

       Feby 16, 1909   S.G. Rogers, Legal Reviewer

       Feby 16, 1909   M. Ketcham, Re-Reviewer

Enlisted Feb. 17, 1862, and honorably discharged May 1, 1863.

Pensioned at $12 per month under Act of June 27-1890.

Present Claim, Act of June 27, 1890

Declaration Special Act of Congress approved Jany 28, 1909 at $24 per month.   Claimant does write.   Certificate not filed.

         -----------------, M.C.

02-19-1909
Act of June 27, 1890
Invalid Series ----------   Cert. No. 105xxxx
Name, Jacob Bowles; Rank, Priv
Service Co K 115th Pa Vol Inf
Agency – Original Roll: ~~Buffalo~~
Transf'd   ------- to Gr 1
M.C.
3" Issue, Class Inc, Fee
Issued Feb 13, 1909. Mailed Feb 19, 1909
Rate and Period, $24, from Jan 28, 1909
Act of June 27, 1890
SPECIAL ACT.

03-19-1909
Act of June 27, 1890
Invalid Series ----------   Cert. No. 105xxxx
Name, Jacob Bowles; Rank, Priv
Service Co K 115th Pa Vol Inf
Agency – Original Roll: ~~Buffalo~~
Transf'd   ------- to Gr 1
INDORSEMENTS
MAR 19 1909 Hon. D. A. Driscoll as per (cofny)
        E.J.B.

03-19-1909
E.J.H.

        March 19, 1909.
        Hon. D. A. Driscoll,
                House of Representatives.
        My dear Mr. Driscoll:
                In reply to your inquiry of the sixteenth instant,
received the seventeenth, relative to the pension case, Certificate
Number 105xxxx, of Jacob Bowles, whose address is 27 Spruce
Street, Buffalo, New York, and who served in Company K, 115th
Pennsylvania Infantry, I have the honor to inform you that he

was formerly pensioned at twelve dollars per month under the Act of June 27, 1890, the maximum rate provided thereunder, and that he is <u>now a pensioner at twenty-four dollars per month by the provisions of a Special Act of Congress</u> approved January 28, 1909.

<u>**There is nothing now pending in this case.**</u>

Very respectfully,

Commissioner.

Finally, the pension quest is finished. With the intervention of Congress, Jacob Bowles now receives the maximum rate. But, ironically, now Jacob is near death. The lifelong effort now gives way to the inevitable. In fact, Jacob Bowles will die in Buffalo, New York, on June 13, 1917. At least, that gives him 8 years to receive the compensation he so intensely pursued.

Once again, moving away from a focus on the pension, we see the intense is set aside, and the mundane taken up. The quest for the pension has borne its fruit. Now the pertinent details of marriage and family need to be updated. Ironically, this very information becomes a part of the basis for questions that arise during the ensuing years.

1915 – Another Marriage Survey

Consistent with their intent to maintain full records on all pensioners, the Bureau of Pensions once again requests marriage and family information. And once again we get a glimpse into the family of Jacob Bowles.

03-20-1915

Department of the Interior, Bureau of Pensions, Washington D.C., January 2, 1915

Sir: Please answer, at your earliest convenience, the questions enumerated below. The information is requested for future use, and it may be of great value to your widow or children. Use this included envelope, which requres no stamp. Very respectfully, G.M.Saltzgaber – Commisioner.

Jacob Bowles, Buffalo, NY, I05xxxx Civ War, 71 Linwood Ave

No 1. Date and place of birth? Answer: I was <u>born in Allegheny City, Pa. 1840 Oct 31st</u>

The name of organizations in which you served?

Answer 115 <u>Pa volunteers company K inlisted 17th of Feb 1862</u>

No 2. What was your post office <u>at enlistment? Answer: Perrysville, Allegheny Co, Pa</u>

No 3. State your wife's full name and her maiden name.

Answer: <u>Adaline Bowles, Pauthie (Panthie?) her maiden name.</u>

No 4. When, where, and by whom were you married?

Answer: <u>1860 at Irwin Station Pa by a justice of Peace, 20th day of August.</u>

No 5. Is there any official or church record of your marriage?

<u>There is no official or church record</u>

No 6. Previously married. No. My dear wife died in 1869, Nov 14. She was my first and only wife untill I married again to my preasant wife in 1886.

No 7. History of present wife: My wife was married before she was married to me. Mr. Samuel Otis in January 13th 1873. Died August 24 1883 in Buffalo NY. He never rendered any cirvis in military. This was her first marage.

No 8. Are you now living with your wife or has there been a separation?

Answer: I am living with my dear wife. Nothing but Deth will seperate us.

No 9. State the names and dates of birth of all your children, living or dead. Answer: I had three sons with my first wife, two are ded. Daniel M. was born feb 12th 1864. Jared B. was born in May 1866 14th. Frank C. was born April 28 1868. To my preasant wife have one step daughter and one step son wich died in infincy. No record of the deth. Ellie my step daughter is married.

March 20th, 1915

Jacob Bowles

1917 - Where is My Pension?

And then, Jacob Bowles dies. In a sense we come full circle. Now the quest builds again – this time for his widow Elizabeth. Can this quest entail the same time frame and agony that Jacob's quest entailed? Elizabeth Bowles comes to the board: "Where is my pension?"

In this section we see the various legal documents pertaining to removing Jacob Bowles from the rolls. Then we see the requirements that Elizabeth must follow in order to qualify for Jacob's pension.

06-26-1917
DECLARATION FOR WIDOW'S PENSION
Act of April 19, 1908
Amended by Act of September 8, 1916
State of New York, County of Erie, SS: On this 26 day of June, 1917, personally appeared before me, a Comm of Deeds within and for the County and State aforesaid, Elizabeth Bowles, who being duly sworn by me according to law, declares that she is 63 years of age and that she was born June 14th, 1854 at St. Catherines, Canada. That she is the widow of Jacob Bowles, who enlisted February 18, 1862 at Pittsburg Pa, under the name of Jacob Bowles, as a Private in Co "K" 115 Pennsylvania Vol. Infantry and was honorably discharged May 1, 1863, having served ninety days or more during the Civil War. That he also served no other service either Military or Naval.

That otherwise than as herein stated said soldier (or sailor) was not employed in the United States service.

That she was married to said soldier May 12th, 1886 under the name
(((1901 Certificate))) of Elizabeth Otis at Fort Erie, Canada, by the Rev. Smith, that she had been previously married; that he had been previously married. Prior marriage of Claimant to Samuel

A. Otis who died August 24, 1883. Prior marriage of soldier to Mary Adell Died June 12, 1869, and that neither she nor said soldier was ever married otherwise than as stated above.

That said soldier died June 13, 1917 at Buffalo N.Y., that she was not divorced from him; and that she has not remarried since his death.

Together, No Minor children.

That she hereby appoints John J. Graves of Buffalo, N.Y. her lawful attorney to prosecute this case.

That she has not heretofore applied for pension, the number of her former claim being 1,05w,www; that said, soldier was a pensioner, the number of his pension certificate being 1,05x,xxx.

~~Mrs. Libbie~~

Samuel R. Glaston, 290 Locust St. Buffalo NY
Elizabeth Bowles
Elinor M. Glaston, 290 Locust St. Buffalo NY
292 Locust St, Buffalo,
Erie Co, NY

Subscribed and sworn to before me this 26 day of June 1917, and I hereby certify that the contents of the above declaration were fully made known and explained to the aplicant before swearing, include the words Mrs. Libbie erased, and the words Elizabeth added, and that I have no interest, direct or indirect, in the prosecution of this claim.

John Shanly, Commisioner of Deeds,
in and for the City of Buffalo

Declaration accepted as a claim under act April 19, 1908, amended by act Sept. 8, 1916. Power of attorney valid as to execution. Chief Law Division per DCH.

07-02-1917
DEPARTMENT OF HEALTH, BUFFALO, N.Y.   No. of Transcript 16xxx
The following is a true copy from the Records of Deaths on file in the Bureau of Vital Statistics, Department of Health, of the

City of Buffalo, N.Y. Transcribed on the July 2, 1917, Francis
E. Fronozak M.D., Health Commisioner, Attest: Franklin C.
Gram, M.D., Registrar of Vital Statistics, Lavin. Place of Death,
County of Erie, City of Buffalo, 92 Ash. Full Name: Samuel A.
Otis. Male, White, Married. Age 31 yrs, 9 days. Occupation
Grape Sugar Mnfr. Birthplace N.S.(Father Jacob Otis, N.S.),
(Mother Eliza Otis, N.S.) Date of Death August 24, 1883
I hereby certify that I attended deceased from July 1 1880 to
Aug. 24 1883, that I last saw him alive on August 24, 1883, and
that death occurred on date shown above, at 7 A.M. The cause
of death was as follows: Phthisis Pulmonalis, duration 3 yrs. –
Arthur M. Barker, M.D., Aug. 24, 1883, Buffalo, N.Y.
Length of residence, in Buffalo 5 yrs. Place of Burial or
removal. North St. Undertaker: Speyser & Manes.
        F.C.Gram, MD

Jul 6-1917
Certificate No. 105xxxx, Class Civil War Invalid,
Pensioner Jacob Bowles, Service K 115 Pa Inf
The Commisioner of Pensions.
Sir,   I have the honor to report that the name of the above-
described pensioner who was last paid at $24, to Apr 4 1917 has
this day been dropped from the roll because of Reported Death
June 13, 1917: Jacob Bowles, Buffalo NY, 105xxxx Civ War,
201 High St,
Very respectfully W. Newelwell, Jul 7 1917

07-07-1917
Pensioner Dropped, Group 1,
Department of the Interior, Bureau of Pensions

07-09-1917
Section One – Received – JUL 9 1917 – Disbursing Office
Deceased 6/13/17
Check No. 4538662
287 W
Special Act. TO LAW DIVISION. Jacob Bowles,
Cert. #105xxxx

07-12-1917
~~G. Allwood~~ Johnston Ex'r., DEPENDENT, No. 110xxxx, K-115,
Act of April 19, 1908
Elizabeth Bowles, 290 Locust St., Buffalo, NY,
Widow, Jacob F. Bowles.
Service K. 115 Pa Inf
Died June 13, 1917, Buffalo, NY & no other claim than I C
105xxxx
July 12, 1917 Clerk: C.D.S.
Application filed: June 30, 1917. Attorney: John J. Graves, P.O.
Buffalo, 327 Chamber of Commerce, NY (atty filed)
Notified July 12, 1917

07-13-1917
DEAD
Act of June 27, 1890
Invalid Series ----------   Cert. No. 105xxxx
Name, Jacob Bowles; Rank, Priv
Service Co K 115th Pa Vol Inf
Agency – Original Roll: ~~Buffalo~~
Transf'd   ------- to Gr 1
DROPPED   JUL 13 1917 FINANCE

08-18-1917
Atty   Death of sol., Mar. to sol., Prior mar. of both more than
once, Death of former consort, Cohab. & non-div., Did former
husb. serve

08-20-1917

Aug 20-17 John J. Graves, Atty, <u>circular for death of sol. mar. to sol. prin mar. of clmt more than once, prin mar. of sol. more than once, cohabitation & non-div. whether former husband served, death of former husband & death of former wife.</u> D.A.G. DEPARTMENT OF THE INTERIOR, BUREAU OF PENSIONS, WASHINGTON – Civil War Division, Wid. Orig. 110xxxx, Elizabeth Bowles, Jacob Bowles, Co. K, 115th Pa.Inf., DAD*JRN, DAG ack.

John J. Graves, Atty., 327 Chamber of Commerce, Buffalo, New York.

Sir:

In this claim, the evidence indicated in paragraph No. 1, 2, 4, 5, 6, 8 should be furnished:

1. <u>Death. A verified copy of the public record, or if no such record exists, the sworn statement of the attending physician, showing the date of the soldier's death.</u> If such evidence can not be obtained, the sworn statement of witnesses having <u>personal knowledge</u> of the facts should be furnished, showing the fact and date of the soldier's death.

2. <u>Marriage. A verified copy of the public or church record of the claimant's marriage to the soldier;</u> or, if no such record exists, the sworn statement of the person who performed the ceremony; or, if that can not be obtained, the sworn statement of two persons who were present at the marriage, showing the date thereof. If the evidence of marriage above indicated can not be obtained, there should be furnished the <u>sworn statement of two persons</u> showing whether the claimant and soldier lived together as husband and wife and were so recognized, and showing where, and how long within the affiant's knowledge they so lived together.

4. If the claimant had been <u>previously married,</u> the fact and date of death or divorce of each former husband should be <u>proved</u>: in case of death, by a <u>verified copy of the public record</u>, or, if no such record exists, by the <u>sworn statement of witnesses</u>; in case of divorce, by a certified copy of the decree of court. If there was

104

only one prior marriage of claimant, the fact should be shown by the sworn statement of witnesses who have known her from the time she became of marriageable age.

5. If the soldier had been previously married, the fact and date of death or divorce of each former wife should be proved; in case of death, by a verified copy of the public record, or, if no such record exists, by the sworn statement of witnesses; in case of divorce, by a certified copy of the decree of court. If there was only one prior marriage of soldier, the fact should be shown by the sworn statement of witnesses who have known him from the time he bacame of marriageable age.

6. The sworn statement of witnesses having knowledge of the facts, showing whether claimant and soldier were ever divorced, and whether they lived together as husband and wife up to the date of the soldier's death.

8. If claimant had been previously married, her sworn statement showing whether any former husband served in the Army or Navy of the United States; and, if so, the designation of such service, and whether any application for pension has been made by herself or any other person based on such service.

A sworn statement may be made before any officer authorized to administer oaths for general purposes. Persons making sworn statements should state their ages, post-office addresses and means of knowledge of the facts to which they testify. Do not fail to inscribe on every paper filed the name and service of the soldier or sailor and the number of the claim to which it relates.

Very respectfully, G. W. Saltzgaber, Commisioner

07-29-1918
Introduced as Evidence:
MARRIAGE CERTIFICATE. Diocese of Niagara – On the 27th day of June 1901 Were Married Jacob F. Bowles of the City of Buffalo N.Y. (Widower) and Elizabeth Oties of the City of Buffalo (Widow) by me, Percy W. Smith, Rector of St. Paul's

Church, Fort Erie, Ont. This Marriage was solemnized between us.   Jacob F. Bowles, Elizabeth Oties
Witnesses: E. Smith, P.A. Smith
I Certify that the above particulars are truly extracted from the Register of Marriages kept in St. Paul's Rectory, Fort Erie, this 29th day of July 1918. D. Russell Smith, Rector of St. Paul's Church, Fort Erie, Ont.

The Reverend D. Russell Smith certifies to me that this is a true and correct transcript taken from the Marriage Records of St. Paul's Church now in his keeping as Pastor. The Church has no official seal. John J. Callahan, Notary Public.
- Certificate on file in Pension Office.

08-19-1918
Town of Elma, Town Clerk's office. To whom it may concern. This is to certify that there are no records of marriages or death prior to eighteen hundred eighty three in this office. Nathaniel Hucker Jr., Town Clerk, Elma Erie County, New York.

08-28-1918
Town of Elma, Town Clerk's office. Walter Dynes, to me personally known, acknowledges that the statements made by him in the attached certificate, are true to the best of his knowledge and belief. Sworn to before me this 19th day of August, 1918. Nathl Hucker, Jr. Notary Public in and for Erie County N.Y. (State of New York, County of Erie – I, John H. Mealh, Clerk of the County of Erie and also Clerk of the Supreme and County Courts for said County, the same being Courts of Record, do hereby certify that Natl. Hucker Jr., whose name is subscribed to the Certificate of the proof, acknowledgment or affidavit, a Notary Public in and for the County of Erie, State of New York, commissioned and sworn and duly authorized by the laws of the State to take and certify the same; and further, that I am well acquainted with the handwriting of such Natl Hucker Jr and verily believe the signature to the said certificate of proof, acknowledgment or

affidavit is genuine. In Testimony whereof, I have hereunto set my hand and affixed the seal of said County and Courts, at Buffalo this 28 day of Aug, 1918. John H. Meahl, Clerk, by Edward J. Clark, Dep. Clerk.)

Elma N.Y., July 24-1918. This is to certify that the church records of the Elma Methodist Episcopal Church contains the following record of a marrage performed by <u>Rev. Geo. M. Harris on Jan 30th 1876 - Samuel A. Otis of Schenectady was married to Elizabeth Olsen of Elma N.Y. on January 24th 30th 1876. George M. Harris, Pastor of M.E. Church, Elma NY. Walter Dynes, Pastor of the Elma M.E. Church, July 24-1918. The Rev G.M. Harris is now pastor of the Methodist-Church at Webster N.Y.</u>

12-21-1918
Village of Fort Erie, Fort Erie, Ontario, Canada.

I have made a diligent search in the records of the Village of Fort Erie for the record of a marriage of Jacob F. Bowles to Elizabeth Otis and <u>I fail to find it.</u> I hereby certify that the records of the Village of Fort Erie, Ont. show <u>no public record of the marriage of Jacob F. Bowles to Elizabeth Otis since the year 1900.</u>
Dated at Fort Erie this 21st day of Dec. 1918   T.M. Dodds, Division Registrar

01-22-1919
Pension Claim No. 110xxxx of Elizabeth Bowles, Widow of Jacob Bowles, Co. 'K' 115th Pa Inf. Affidavit of Barbara A. Nelson and Catharine Lerner. State of New York, County of Erie – SS: In the matter of the pension claim No. 110xxxx of Elizabeth Bowles, widow of Jacob Bowles Co. "K" 115th Pa. Inf.

<u>Barbara A. Nelson, aged 73 years, residing at Elma Centre, New York,</u> county of Erie, and <u>Catharine Lerner, aged 56 years, residing at Depew, County of Erie</u> and State of New York, being duly sworn according to law declare that they are <u>sisters of</u>

the claimant and have always been in a position to know much about her affairs both socially and otherwise, having always lived near her. They can certify that she was not previously married before she married Samuel A. Otis her first husband, and we know that she lived with him continuously without separation or divorce till the date of his death, August 24, 1883, and did not again re-marry until she married the soldier with whom she lived continuously from date of marriage without separation or divorce to the date of his death, which occurred Jun 13, 1917, and since his death, she has not again re-married. All of which is personally well known to deponents. That we have no interest directly or indirectly in the prosecution of this claim.

Barbara A. Nelson; Catharine Lerner.
Subscribed and sworn to before me on this 22nd day of January 1919.

John J. Callahan, Notary Public

02-06-1919
GENERAL AFFIDAVIT – State of Pennsylvania, County of Allegheny SS: In the matter of record in this City, as you will note by the enclosed statement.
Yours very truly, J.F. Binders, Chief Clerk.
Certified Copy of Death Record, City of Pittsburgh, Department of Public Health, Bureau of Infections Diseases – Vital

Mary Adell Bowles – No record of Deaths previous to July 1, 1870. J.A. Beck, Clerk.

08-01-1919
No. 110x,xxx. General Affidavit. Case of Elizabeth Bowles, Widow of Jacob Bowles,
Co "K" 115th Pa Inf. Affidavit of Frank R. Price, date of execution: August 1, 1919.

Ongoing Scrambled & Scandaled Details

Jacob Bowles, enlisted while a shoemaker, discharged with disability, spent years attempting to collect a pension. Eventually he left the shoemaker's profession to become a painter. Upon his death, his widow made application for his pension. The pension board, legitimately, made every effort to verify that this was a single claim – that there was no prior wife who had applied for pension and that his relationship with his current wife, upon his death, was valid.

This seems to be a straightforward enough effort, with the likely outcome being the normal processing of the pension and passing it on to his rightful widow. Little could we know that this is where truth takes even more circuitous turns and further surpasses fiction. And this is where the life of Jacob Bowles makes itself so difficult to track (at least for one conspicuous period of time) under the normal records available, (namely 10-year census records) to the amateur researcher of genealogy.

Just as a quick exercise, let's go through the stated residences of Jacob Bowles during the time he was pursuing a disability pension. In May of 1863 he was stated as 24 years old, a resident of Pittsburg, Pennsylvania. In February of 1873 he is 33 years old, a resident of Ridgway, Elk County, Pennsylvania. He claims a wife named Mary A. "Pochie?" whom he married at Westmoreland in August, 1860. (Note, he married before his enlistment.) He claims 3 sons and a step-daughter, born 1864, 1865, 1868 and 1874. Note that the births of his sons are subsequent to his time in the army! These would be the sons of his first wife. In January of 1886, he is 46 years old and a resident of Buffalo, County of Erie, State of New York. I am highly suspicious that by the beginning of 1886 he was already acquainted with the woman who was to become his second wife, and she was instrumental in applying pressure to get him to pursue the pension payments.

By December of 1895 it appears he has moved again, his address being 44 Spruce St.,Buffalo, NY. In 1896 he is 55 years old, still living in Buffalo. Jacob appears somewhat more stable now; in January of 1901 he is 60 years old and lists a post office address of 27 Spruce St., Buffalo, NY. He is now a contract painter.

Now this seems to be a set of data that shouldn't be too difficult to track down in the midst of the US census records. Here is a fairly stable family, although needy, that finds itself settled down with a second wife mostly in Erie County in New York. But, surprise! As the Pensions Board pares down the information pertaining to this widow of Jacob Bowles, we get some surprising testimony from one of his sons! It appears this was not the happiest of families!

A Surprising Perspective

07-30-1920
Case of Elizabeth Bowles,
No. 110xxxx
On this 30 day of July, 1920, at Pittsburgh county of Allegheny, State of Pennsylvania, before me, Theodore Tallmadge, a Special Examiner of the Bureau of Pensions, personally appeared <u>Daniel M. Bowles</u>, who, being by me first duly sworn to answer truly all interrogatories propounded to her during this special examination of aforesaid claim for pension, deposes and says:

My age is 56 years, born Feb. 12, 1864; Occupation:-Forman painter; Address:- No. 255 Seneca St., Turtle Creek, Penna.

I am son of Jacob F. Bowles by his wife Mary, maiden name not recalled, hold on it was Jacklett. I recall the fact of death of my mother in Allegheny, Pa., on Perrysville Ave., when I was five years of age, I do not know the date, and was buried in a Cemetery on Mt. Washington, -part of Pittsburgh- the name of which I do not recall though I recollect going there to the funeral and going across the two bridges, one at the Point, and down and around the hill. I know of no brothers or sisters of my mother who now survive. I was not taught in childhood as to my mother's people and hence never learned.

I am the eldest of three brothers, Jared B. and Frank C., both are dead. There were no sisters except one who died before I was born.

I was taught that my father was reared in Jacktown or Irwin or in that neighborhood. The only authority for that statement is the fact that as a boy he worked in the coal mines there. My father's father was John Bowles, he had been a miner but lived in East Liberty in my knowledge of him and drove a stage between Irwin and Pittsburgh. I did know my Grandmother Bowles but have forgotten all about her. Those born to my father's parents were Daniel Bowles, Henry Bowles, Brian Bowles, and one daughter Nancy Bowles besides my father Jacob. The boys are all dead but Nancy married Ralph Taylor and is a widow and lives with her daughter, Frances Holden of Brookline, a part of Pittsburgh.

My recollection following the death of my mother is that the family went to Meadville, Pa., taking the children, and there he got a woman to take care of the family. I believe her name Hannah Nelson, she had one child herself, a boy Samuel, who took our name and was taught that he was a brother. He was younger than me. It was during the oil excitement at Meadville that we were there and then we all went to Oil City, that is, my father Hannah Nelson and the four boys. We did not stay there

111

very long but went to Buffalo, N.Y. when I was about six years old, six years past, and the same household was there, remaining not over a year. Then we came back to Allegheny, the same household, remaining about two years, and then the same household went to Tyrone Pa. for about two years or a little more, and then the same household went to Reynoldsville, Pa., that was during the panic of 1873 and 1874 and were there about three years, and from there the same household went to Lock Haven, Pa., but did not remain there over a year and a half or two years, think I was then around about 10 or 11 years old. Then the same household returned to Allegheny and remained until I was about 14 years of age when we, the same household went to Buffalo N.Y. and stayed there until the home was broken up, it was when I was 17 years of age that the household was broken up. Yes that would be about 1881. I then went for myself. The two brothers of mine and Hannah Nelson's son remained with her and in Buffalo and I remained in Buffalo but with neither her nor my father. My father at that time, **when the household was broken up** went to living in Buffalo with the woman who I suppose is the claimant in this case, **deserting** the woman who had been with him during the years the children were small and who we were taught to call "Mother." I knew no different. I recall this woman's name only as "Liz" as she was called and fail to recognize either Olson or Otis as her name. This "Liz" had a daughter Ellie who I knew. Ellie was presumedly a legitimate child and her mother was a widow when my father went to live with her when our household already referred to was broken up. The home was on Michigan St. when it was broken up, father leaving there

   Daniel M. Bowles

Case of Elizabeth Bowles, No. 110xxxx, Deposition of Daniel M. Bowles, continued, sheet 2

for this woman "Liz" with whom he went to live in the East End somewhere, in the vicinity of Jefferson St., where I found out her relations, her sisters, lived, and some are still living there. I can not give their names. I continued to reside in Buffalo until I was past 21 years of age, and saw my father not very often, but knew where he was living. Hannah Nelson continued to remain in Buffalo while I lived there, residing on Clinton St. near Elm the last I knew, she was then keeping house and had her son with her, my brothers having left and were taking care of themselves in Buffalo. Hannah Nelson was up the time I left Buffalo at 21 years of age past, going by the name of Nelson. Her son Samuel later after the home was broken up took the name of Nelson and was a drayman by occupation. With Hannah Nelson in Buffalo at the time I left there, there was living with her, her sister Minnie Taylor, a grass widow, but Nelson was her maiden name. Once since then I learned that Hannah had gone back to Eldred, McKean Co., Pa., a place where we had lived in our moving from place to place which among other places where we stayed so short a time that I did not think of mentioning in the first part of this statement, but I did not understand that she remained there. I practically lost all track of Hannah Nelson when I left Buffalo, N.Y., and even could not locate her there when I returned there a year or two after I left as already stated. I do not know whether she is living or dead. Hannah had a brother Samuel Nelson a painter who resided in Buffalo when I left there and for two or three years afterwards, residing on the East side of Buffalo but can not give further location, but I have lost all track of him too. I know of no other relatives. I have been in this section for over 30 years and in that time have paid very little attention to those at Buffalo. It is proper to state that upon my first marriage at the age of 29 years there was a partial reconciliation between father and I, only such as might be attributed to the relationship and not such as relieved him of the censure that I believed was due him for deserting the woman who had reared his orphan children and who had taken his name and whose son Samuel also had taken his name and who as far as I then knew or ever had reason to believe was to all intents and purposes my father's wife. After the separation of my father from Hannah Nelson I learned from her that she had lived with my father without a marriage ceremony having been performed.

My father never made any explanation of the matter. I learned in
some way that the child Samuel of Hannah Nelson was an
illegitimate child and so far as I ever heard or knew, she had no
husband before she bacame my father's consort and at that time
we children were taught to call her "Mother" and to this day I
resent my father's conduct toward this woman who was a
devoted mother to us and in all respects conducted herself as a
true wife to my father.

There were no children born to Hannah Nelson while
living with my father. However I know that **they occupied the
same room and bed and that they held themselves as
husband and wife,** and there was no claim made that she was
his housekeeper or that her relations were other than that of a
legal wife to my father.

I wish I could set you right that you might locate Hannah
Nelson but I do not know where to suggest. I am naturally
opposed to this woman who usurped the position of the wife
Hannah as not entitled to this pension. Samuel Glaston who
married Ellie daughter of "Liz" knows this woman "Liz" but not
Hannah. Asked who would know Hannah or knew when my
father lived with her as a husband, I am unable to mention same.

I can not recall living on Genesee or Michigan St. with
my father and Hannah. Since you have read what is shown by
the Buffalo City Directory for the several years from 1883, I am
able to now state that I remained in Buffalo after I was 21 years
of age for the name "Bowles, Danies M. piano finisher, 77 Swan
St.," appearing in the 1890 directory refers to me as to
occupation and residence, though I do not fix the year except as
you say it appears in the 1890 City Directory. Jared Bowles
referred to in your statement from the Directory is my brother
Jared who remained in Buffalo until his death, having married
before his death, and was survived by a widow, name not known,
and he died over 25 years   Daniel M. Bowles
Case of Elizabeth Bowles, No. 110xxxx, Deposition of Daniel
M. Bowles, continued, sheet 3

ago. My brother Frank left Buffalo before I did and died in Jacksonville, Fla., having married in Pittsburgh where he came from Buffalo.

Samuel Nelson brother of Hannah who I have mentioned was a painter and married but had no children to my knowledge or the (erased) and can not state the name of his wife.

The name of my mother comes to me now "Josephine" and not "Mary" as appears in the first of this statement; Also the name "Otis" comes to me as the surname of the woman "Liz" herein referred to.

I attended my father's funeral in Buffalo three years ago this last June, and at that time this woman "Liz" was there and from appearances seemed to have assumed the position of a widow. I made no inquiries at the time and since then she has sought my assistance to secure this pension but I have refused to answer her letters. I really believe that "Liz" does not know that I know the part she took in **coming between my father and the wife Hannah** and caused this separation, and if I should have written her at all I would have been inclined to tell her some of these things which she does not think I know. This woman "Liz" knew my father was actually living with Hannah and that she was his wife as far as known to people in that community, and nevertheless, knowing of the obligation existing between my father and Hannah, this woman "Liz" designedly and equally to blame with my father, **broke up the home by enticing** my father away from Hannah. This is why I dislike this woman.

Asked as to my knowledge or information concerning any marriage of my father I can only say that I assume he was married to my mother, and I likewise assumed he was next married to Hannah but Hannah told me herself that they were not married by a ceremony. I know nothing about my father's marriage to "Liz", he referred to her however as his wife after he left Hannah, **just the same as he had referred to Hannah when he lived with her**. These two women, Hannah and "Liz" are the only women I have any knowledge of my father living with in what was claimed to be the marital relation. I never heard of any divorce between Hannah and my father, but I was compelled to accept her statement that they were naver married when, upon the separation, she, Hannah, resumed the name of Nelson, and informed me there was no marriage ceremony between them.

I have no financial interest in this claim; I have heard the foregoing statement read and it is correct.

Daniel M. Bowles, Deponent

Sworn to and subscribed before me on this the 30 day of July 1920 and I certify that the contents were fully made known to the deponent before signing.

Theodore Tallmadge, Special Examiner

Let's look at Daniel Bowles' recollections. He was the son of Jacob Bowles by his first wife, name fuzzy, maybe Mary or Josephine Jacklet or Pochie. Jacob remembers it as Adeline, which could easily be interpreted as "Mary Adell." Daniel was born about 1864. She died when he was 5 years old, about 1869. He remembers the cemetery.

1. *1869, The family moved to Meadville, Pa. A woman took care of the family, named Hannah Nelson, who had one child.*
2. *(?) Soon all moved to Oil City, not for long.*
3. *1870? went to Buffalo, NY, for not more than a year.*
4. *1870? came back to Allegheny for about 2 years.*
5. *1872? Went to Tyrone, Pa. for about 2 years or a little more.*
6. *1873? Went to Reynoldsville (during the panic of 1873-1874) and were there for about 3 years.*
7. *1875? Went to Lock Haven, Pa. but did not remain at most for 2 years.*
   Age approximately 10-11 years, putting it at 1874-1875.
8. *Returned to Allegheny and remained until about 1878 (14 years old).*

9. *Same household went to Buffalo, NY, staying there until the home was broken up – I was about 17 (1881).*

10. *Dates and actual times are not surprisingly confused. Most of this occurred while he was under the age of 14.*

11. *We now can see some very concrete reasons that this period of time passed without any request for a pension from James Bowles. He may have been too busy chasing get-rich-schemes to settle down and pursue a pension.*

12. *All this time Hannah Nelson and her son were with the family.*

13. *The children called Hannah Nelson "mother" and she shared a bed with his father.*

14. *When the household was "broken up," his father left them to go live with "Liz."*

15. *Hannah had gone back to Eldred, McKean Co., Pa., where the family had lived for a very short time.*

16. *"After the separation of my father from Hannah Nelson I learned from her that she had lived with my father without a marriage ceremony having been performed."*

17. *to this day I resent my father's conduct toward this woman who was a devoted mother to us and in all respects conducted herself as a true wife to my father.*

18. *This woman "Liz" knew my father was actually living with Hannah and that she was his wife as far as known to people in that community, and nevertheless, knowing of the obligation existing between my father and Hannah, this woman "Liz" designedly and equally to blame with my father, broke up the home by enticing my father away from Hannah. This is why I dislike this woman.*

A Timeline for Study and Evaluation

That's a general overview of Daniel's testimony. In a more rigorous manner, let us attempt to put together a timeline of the events involving Jacob Bowles and his family. I ask you to diligently put on your investigator's cap and sift through whatever clues are here to bring enlightenment:

1840   Oct 31, Jacob Bowles born in Allegheny City, Pa.

1850   The family of Jason Bowles (who was the father of Jacob Bowles) appears in   the PA census, <u>Allegheny County, Reserve Township</u>.

Jason Bowles	35, m	Laborer Pa	father of Jacob
Mary	36, f		mother of Jacob
Daniel	11, m	brother	
Jacob	9, m		our protagonist
Brian	7, m	brother	
Nancy A.	4, f	sister	
Henry	2, m	brother	
Martin	1, f (sic)	brother(?)	

1860   Jacob Bowles and Hannah Nelson located in censuses:

1860 PA Census, Elk County, Jones

John Nelson	55, m	NY	Carpenter
Mary	43, f	NY	
Arnaline	14, f	NY	"Hannah Nelson"
John L.	9, m	NY	
Miennie	6, f	Pa	Minnie -> Taylor
Saml	3, m	Pa	Samuel Nelson

1860 PA Census, Allegheny, East Birmingham

Jacob Bowles	21, m	Pa	Shoemaker

08-20-1860   Jacob Bowles marries Adeline (Mary Adell) <Pochie, Poeline>, Previn Town, Westmoreland County, Pa. "My first marriage was in 1860 – 20th of August, Previn Town, Westmoreland Co, Pa." "Adaline Bowles, Pauthie (or Panthie) her maiden name. 1860 at Irwin Station, Pa by a justice of Peace, 20th day of August." From Frances R. Holden: "I have heard my mother speak in times past of the mother of the child Daniel by referring to her as 'Addie.'"

1862	02-24 Jacob Bowles mustered into service as a Pvt, at Harrisburg, Pa.

1862   02-24   Jacob Bowles mustered into service as a Pvt, at
Harrisburg, Pa.
Regimental History, PENNSYLVANIA, 115TH
INFANTRY, On Feb. 27, 1862, it left for Washington and
was assigned Gen. Locke.
05-31   Jacob Bowles injured at Fair Oaks, Virginia ->
Yorktown hosp, -> Sugar Grove -> Hestonville

1863   04-25   Jacob Bowles found incapable of service due to
Scrofulous Diathesis & Constant Debility
05-02   Jacob Bowles applies for disability (invalid
pension), appoints Laughlin & Maddox as Attys.
Residency Pittsburg.

1863   May, approx.   Daniel Bowles conceived! Interesting
date. How soon after Jacob returned from the service?

1864   02-12   birth of Daniel M. Bowles

1866   05-14   birth of Jared B. Bowles

1868   04-28   birth of Frank C. Bowles

1869   06-12   alleged date of death of Jacob Bowles' first wife.
Some list it back to May of 1868. There appears to be more
verification of the 1869 date.

Testimony of Daniel: "I recall the fact of death of my
mother in Allegheny, Pa, on Perrysville Ave., when I was
five years of age....
buried in a Cemetery on Mt. Washington –part of
Pittsburgh- the name of which I do not recall though I
recollect going there to the funeral and going across the two
bridges, one at the Point, and down and around the hill."
Theodore Tallmadge – search of cemeteries, 1867-1871.
"It is inferred that the Cemetery referred to by witness must
have been a semi private burial ground and has long since
passed out of existence."

1870   *Jacob Bowles and Hannah located in censuses:*
There seems quite a puzzle here, as "Mary" is
still listed with Jacob Bowles in 1870, and
Hannah is still with the Nelsons.
06-04   1870 PA Census, Erie County, Corry

Jacob Bowles	29, m	Shoemaker	Pennsylvania
Mary	21, f	Keeping house	France
	(sister of Mary Adeline? Adeline? Mary Adell?)		
Daniel	6, m		Pa
Jared	4, m		Pa

```
Frank          2, m                      Pa
07-29   1870 PA Census, Elk County, Benzinger (P.O. St.
        Mary's) (found by manual search)
Nelson, John   67, m   Carpenter        New York
        Maria   42, f   Keeping House    New York
        *Arnaline 24, f                   New York
        John L. 19, m   Painter          Penna
        Samuel  13, m                    Penna
        Samuel  4, m                     Penna
                (son of Arnaline(Hannah))
        Tyler, Robert    35, m   Painter  Conn
        Hellen  18, m(sic)       Keeping House   Penna
        Minny   10/12,f                   Penna
```

1869 – 1875 "The Oil Years"

> *Meadville, Pa. Hannah Nelson there. (~1869)*
> *Oil City.*
> *Buffalo, NY. (~1870)*
> *Allegheny (~1870)*
> *Tyrone, Pa. (~1872)*
> *Reynoldsville (panic of 1873-1874) (~1873)*
> *Ridgeway*

2-7-1873   <u>*Request for pension made; Pa, Elk County;*</u>
            <u>*Ridgeway. On Mill Street.*</u>
            Corroborating information: Has R.S. Taylor of
            Ridgway as witness. ((So at least by 02-07-1873
            Jacob Bowles is "in Ridgway," Nellie Nelson
            Taylor (sister of 'Hannah') is in Ridgway
            and Jacob Bowles knows Robert Taylor well
            enough to have him as a witness. Based on 1870
            census, it is likely that the rest of the Nelson
      family
            is also in Ridgway.))

1873   02-07 Jacob Bowles in Ridgway,
            Elk Co, Pa (Mill Street)
            Robert Taylor in Ridgway, Elk Co, Pa
            (Note – Ridgway next to <u>Benzinger</u>,
            see 1870 census)

Reynoldsville (= <u>Winslow</u>), Pa <~3 yrs>
LockHaven, Pa   <1 ½ to 2 yrs>
Allegheny, Pa
Lock Haven (~1875). Daniel was 10-11 years old.
Allegheny (until ~1878). 14 years old.
Buffalo, NY. (until ~1881)

1880   Census Records located

1880 PA Census, Winslow, Jefferson

Bowles, Jacob	m, 40	Pa,Pa,Pa	Painter
Hannah E.	f, 33	NY,NY,NY	**
Daniel M.	m, 16	Pa	
Jared B.	m, 14	Pa	
Samuel R.	m, 13	Pa	**child of Hannah
Frank C.	m, 12	Pa	
Taylor, Robert	m, 47	Conn,Conn,Pa	Painter
Minnie	f, 27	Pa	
Minnie	f, 11	Pa	

1880 PA Census, McKean, Eldred

Nelson, Samuel	m, 22	Pa,NY,NY	fireman in sawmill
Rosy	f, 19		
Samuel	m, 11/12		
John R.	m, 74	father	NY
Mary	f, 52	mother	NY

1880   Jacob Bowles' family are w/ Hannah in Winslow, Jefferson Co, Pa
Robert Taylor & Minnie next door to Jacob Bowles in Winslow, Jefferson Co, Pa
John & Mary Nelson w/ Hannah's brother Samuel in Eldred, McKean Co, Pa

Buffalo, NY (abt. 1881)

"Same household went to Buffalo, NY, staying there until the home was broken up – I was about 17 (1881)".

1881   In the memory of Samuel Bowles, Elizabeth was in the process of breaking up the family in 1881. (This was more likely about 1883 to 1886).

08-24-1883 Death of Samuel A. Otis. Elizabeth Bowles: "We then lived in this City on Ash Street when he died. We lived near the crossing of Sycamore. He died of consumption."

1883   Jacob Bowles' family @ 209 Genessee Street in Buffalo
1884   Jacob Bowles' family @ 589 Michigan Street in Buffalo
1885   *"House broken up"*
        Jacob & Jareed @ 24 Sycamore in Buffalo
        Samuel & Hannah (Bowles) @ 189 Michigan in Buffalo
        Daniel Bowles @ 84 Swan in Buffalo

Subsequent pension requests and correspondence:
1-27-1886   Pension request from Buffalo, Erie county, NY.
Address 30 Exchange St, Buffalo, NY.
2-24-1886 Address 33 Exchange St, Buffalo, NY.
1887   Jacob Bowles @ 1491 Main St. w/ Elizabeth & her Parents
        Daniel & Jared @ 84 Swan Street
2-20-1888 Address 33 Exchange St, Buffalo, NY.
1890   Jacob @ 298 Cedar Street
        Jacob @ 69 Delaware Ave <1890 surviving soldiers special census>
        Daniel @ 77 Swan Street
        Minnie Taylor (w/ Hannah Nelson & Samuel) @ 349 Clinton Street,
1891   Jacob @ 298 Cedar Street
1892   Jared @ 429 William Street
1895   Buffalo, NY.   : ***Physicians' Board***
12-18-1895 Address 44 Spruce St, Buffalo, NY. ***Lockport.***
03-11-1896 Address 44 Spruce St, Buffalo, NY.
01-28-1901 Address 27 Spruce St, Buffalo, NY.
05-14-1901 Address 27 Spruce St, Buffalo, NY.
07-03-1901 Address 27 Spruce St, Buffalo, NY. ***Buffalo.***
10-12-1901 Address 27 Spruce St, Buffalo, NY.
11-06-1901 Address 27 Spruce St, Buffalo, NY. ***Springville.***
10-01-1902 Address 27 Spruce St, Buffalo, NY. ***Lockport.***
04-11-1903 Address 27 Spruce St, Buffalo, NY.
04-22-1903 Address 27 Spruce St, Buffalo, NY. ***Buffalo.***
09-30-1903 Address 27 Spruce St, Buffalo, NY.
03-02-1904 Address 27 Spruce St, Buffalo, NY. ***Batavia.***
        Note that a reasonable randomness has been applied by
the Pension Board concerning which board of Physicians does
the examination.   Lockport -> Buffalo -> Springville ->
Lockport -> Buffalo -> Batavia.
01-28-1909 Full pension of $24/month approved by Congress.
*03-19-1909 **Case closed, federal intervention**.*

06-26-1917 Erie County, state of NY.
07-06-1917 Jacob Bowles dropped from the roll because of
            Death 06-13-1917.
09-08-1920 Elizabeth Bowles approved for Accrued pension
            Elizabeth Bowles receives accrued widow's
            pension of $990.
1934   Death of Elizabeth Bowles on 05-29-1934. Pension
            canceled, last payment of $36/month to April 30, 1934.
            Final end of the line.

Human Values

Daniel Bowles puts more faith in human relationships and commitments than the existence of a piece of paper. He is irate that if anyone is due a pension, it should not be some "gold-digger" woman who broke up his family, but rather the woman who spent years of her time as his "mother" and his father's consort. His major problem now is that he cannot produce Hannah – he has totally lost track of her. Fascinatingly, he is not even aware that his "step-mother" Hannah is in fact the sister of his biological mother. What a complicated web! His mother dies, her sister comes to care for the children for at least 10 years. And then, here comes Elizabeth to usurp her position.

Now, given Daniel Bowles' take on the matter, what might we expect as an end result of all this? Is Liz as manipulative as he seems to think? Has she wormed her way into his father's life primarily in order to benefit herself? It is at this point that we begin to weave in some of the other testimony being accumulated by the pension board.

1. *August, 1919. Elizabeth Bowles provides sworn testimony of Frank Price that Jacob Bowles was a single man from at least 1886, until he married Elizabeth in 1901. (Well, actually married in 1886, but what does Frank Price know?)*

2. *Elizabeth Bowles provides a record of death for Jacob Bowles. She also admits there is no public record of their marriage. As to the death of his first wife, there is no public record but instead she submits a Bible record.*

3. *She provides a public record of the death of her first husband, in 1883. (Note that Daniel's recollection of his family's breakup dates to 1881!)*

   The pension board, in October of 1919, raises an interesting issue. They point out that in the 1915 marriage circular Jacob stated the date of his marriage to Elizabeth was 1886. Then why was it necessary to marry her again in 1901 and to go to Canada to have the ceremony performed when both were residents of Buffalo, NY? "The claimant alleged in her statement before me that she was first married to the soldier by a Captain of the Salvation Army in Buffalo in 1886, and was to have been given a certificate of marriage, but the Captain disappeared and there being no public record of said marriage, she decided to have soldier go to Fort Erie, Canada, where they were ceremonially married in 1901."

4. *Claimant alleges no marriage prior to her marriage to Samuel A. Otis Jan's 30, 1876 and proves the marriage by copy of church record. The soldier however, gives the date of claimant's former marriage (in 1915 circular) as Jany 13, 1873 and refers to a living step-daughter, Mrs. Ellie Glaston, who in a former marriage circular (1901) he states was born April 16, 1874. It is not shown who was the father of said step-daughter if claimant was married*

to Otis in 1876. There is evidently something not disclosed as to his life during the interval and a special examination is desired to determine whether there was more than one prior marriage by either. Who were the parents of the stepdaughter referred to as born in 1874?

5. *In 1920 the Pension Board, Special Examination Division, tried to establish historical records of Elizabeth Olson/Otis in Elma, NY. There was no success.*

6. *There is a discrepancy in the marriage date for Samuel Otis and Elizabeth Olson. These are either January 13, 1873 or January 30, 1876. The 1876 date appears to be the correct one.*

7. *Elizabeth admits that the difference in marriage dates calls into question the legitimacy of her daughter's birth: "You have called my attention to the date of marriage to Samuel A. Otis as January 30, 1876, which would indicate that my daughter Mrs. Glaston was born before that date if she will be 45 on the 16th day of this month. I will say I may be mistaken as to her age, and will try to look up the Bible record and baptismal records and show to you later. My said daughter was not born out of wedlock or prior to my ceremonial marriage with Otis. Otis was her father. I cant explain discrepancies in date of marriage and birth of daughter Ellie."*

8. *The Bible Elizabeth provides has some discrepancies. MARRIAGES: "Samuel A. Otis --- Elizabeth Olson, was married by Rev. Mr. Harris January 30, 1873." (written under above the words "Jan. 31, 1873", and the figure 3 written over an erasure. Otherwise the records appears genuine, Special Examiner) "Jacob F. Bowles --- Elizabeth Otis, was married by Percy W. Smith May 12, 1886, Rector of Fort Erie Ont." (The name Percy W. Smith was written over an*

erasure, Special Examiner). *"I can't explain the erasures in either of the above named records."*

9. *"I do solemly swear that Ellie was born after I was ceremonially married to Samuel A. Otis and he was her father."* *(Subsequent investigation will show that, in fact, Ellie was born before the marriage.)*

The Special Examiner was very detailed in his search for information on this matter. *In May of 1920 he asserts:* *To more fully determine claimant's social status I made a search of the State Census Reports for the Town of Elma, Erie County, N.Y. for 1875, and found as follows:*

"Census of Inhabitants living in the Second Election District of Elma in the County of Erie, N.Y. on the first day of June 1875", *as enumerated on the 23 day of June 1875, by Timothy Clifford, Enumerator.* *Note that this is not the 10-yearly federal census, but rather a specific state census for Erie County in New York.*

No. 1xx, Page xx.

Name of every person whose place of abode was in the Family on the 1ˢᵗ day of June 1875.	*Age.*	*Relation to head of family.*	*Married or Single.*	***B**irthplace*
"Baltazar Olson, (head of family)"	*"54"*	*"Married"*		*"Germany"*
"Jana Olson"	*"51"*	*"Wife"*	*do*	*do*
"Elizabeth Olson"	*"21"*	*"Daughter"*	*"Single"*	*N. Y.*
"Catharine Olson"	*"18"*	*"Daughter"*	*"Single"*	*N. Y.*
"Mary Olson"	*"15"*	*"Daughter"*	*"Single"*	*N. Y.*
"Fanny Olson"	*"12"*	*"Daughter"*	*"Single"*	*N. Y.*
"Dietrich Olson"	*"10"*	*"Son"*	*"Single"*	*N. Y.*
"Ellie Olson"	*" 1"*	*"Daughter"*	*"Single"*	*N. Y.*

Here is proof Ellie Olson was living prior to 1875. *"The above is conclusive that the child was born out of wedlock, and prior to marriage to Otis in 1876."*

1. *A fascinating trail of details emerges from the testimony of the sister of Jacob Bowles. It ties together some of the memories of Daniel Bowles, as well as lending some question to others. Nancy Ann Taylor, nee Bowles, was born to a father Jason and mother Mary, into a family of 5 boys and 2 girls. She knew of the first wife of Jacob Bowles, and says she died about 1867-1868.*
2. *The lady who stepped in to care for the children was **not a stranger**. She was, in fact, the sister of Jacob's first wife!*
3. *Jacob then was a shoemaker, had his own shoe shop. Later he went into the painting business, house painter. When he left Allegheny he went to Buffalo. According to his sister, "He was a painter there and his wife took charge of the church after they were married there. I do not know what induced him to go to Buffalo. I do not know of him living elsewhere after leaving Allegheny where his wife died until he went to Buffalo. I know nothing about Jacob being in the oil country or following that business or being at Ridgeway, and don't think he was." (Here her testimony conflicts with that of Daniel).*

In August of 1920, the Special Examiner embarks on a quest to find out more about Hannah Nelson, who was the step-mother of Jacob Bowles' children for so many years (according to Daniel).

1. *To Mr. Samuel Nelson, Buffalo, NY: "Hannah Nelson is said to have had a brother named Samuel Nelson, and a son named Samuel Nelson, and a sister named Minnie Taylor, and I would like to find any of*

them who are now living, and finding your name in the City directory has prompted me to write you in the hope you may be able to give me some information about these parties, even though you may not be related to them.

2. *The response is disappointing: "Don't know of eny such persons.   Yours, Saml. C. Nelson, 124 Northland Ave"*

3. *Apparently, every effort of the Special Examiner turns up fruitless.*
    And Elizabeth Bowles appears to be generous: "If you can find Hannah and learn she was married to the soldier and was never divorced then I would say give the pension to her, as I would not want it if not legally and lawfully entitled to it.   I have no other testimony to offer in support of my claim."

4. *Through one unfortunate oversight the proof of Daniel Bowles' claim about Hannah Nelson was missed.   In 1880, instead of being in Buffalo for the census, Jacob Bowles and his family were in Pennsylvania.   This census information establishes the existence of Daniel's step-mother: After such intensive research by both N.B. Miller and by Theodore Tallmadge, it is a shame that with one oversight this research gets dropped.   In Pennsylvania, at least the partial validity of Daniel M. Bowles' testimony would have been established.   I still believe it would not have led to useful results, as Ms. Nelson, brother Samuel, son Samuel, and sister Minnie seem to vanish into thin air anyway. –*

1880 PA Census, Winslow, Jefferson

Bowles, Jacob	m, 40	Pa,Pa,Pa	Painter
Hannah E.	f, 33	NY,NY,NY	
Daniel M.	m, 16	Pa	
Jared B.	m, 14	Pa	
Samuel R.	m, 13	Pa	child of Hannah

<pre>
         Frank C.   m, 12   Pa
    Taylor, Robert   m, 47   Conn,Conn,PaPainter
         Minnie   f, 27   Pa
         Minnie   f, 11   Pa
    1880 PA Census, McKean, Eldred
    Nelson, Samuel m, 22   Pa,NY,NY fireman in sawmill
         Rosy   f, 19
         Samuel   m, 11/12
    John R.   m, 74   father NY
         Mary   f, 52   mother NY
</pre>

5. Eventually, the widow's pension was granted to Elizabeth Bowles. None of the investigative efforts had borne sufficient fruit to change this outcome.

04-19-1920	*Reputed Bible of Elizabeth Bowles 'and now produce my old Bible… and believe my respective husbands did the writing in the records in which each figured.' ((Note – I don't think there would be any reason for Jacob Bowles to have written anything in this Bible record, and certainly not to indicate 1886 as his marriage at Fort Erie, and to write it in Elizabeth's Bible. And why would he make the entry about his first wife in Elizabeth's Bible? That has nothing to do with her. And why is it nearly identical to the entry in Jacob's alleged Bible?' "Mrs. Mary Adell Bowles departed this life June 12th, A.D. 1869." All the evidence seems to point to Elizabeth Bowles using the Bible as a platform to establish the "truth" of her own claims.*

Truth and Fiction

Throughout his life Jacob Bowles experienced an incredible tension between truth and fiction. As previously mentioned, he found himself at a point where his truth was the fiction of the Pension Board, and vice versa. In retrospect, the facts of his pursuit seem to defy reality. And yet, we have the records in hand of his interaction with the board.

Then we encounter the testimonies of others in the case, especially those of Daniel Bowles and Elizabeth Bowles. These are given under oath and purport to be truth. And yet, how much weight can we give to the validity of the memories, or of the entries in the Bible. Are there any solid answers available here?

Can we condemn Elizabeth Olson Otis Bowles, as Daniel Bowles wanted to? Think of what this poor woman was trying to do. She didn't want to hurt her family – she had a reputation to protect. For goodness sake, she was an upright citizen – a hard worker at the hospital, and "his wife took charge of the church after they were married there" (Nancy Ann Taylor concerning Jacob and Elizabeth.) How could she let all of that go? She must have been properly married before bearing Ellie, she must have been properly married to Jacob Bowles from the very beginning in 1886. Any other admission would damage those who trusted her – what she did was ultimately for their good. Probably, she was always "sweet Elizabeth" to the family, the one who always did the best, the one who always encouraged everyone else.

As another aspect of fact and fiction, note how many people are testifying to "facts" concerning events surrounding Jacob Bowles, when in fact they are only repeating what someone, usually Elizabeth, has told them. Note Frances Holden's statement (07-27-1920), concerning the death of Jacob Bowles' first wife – "the details of her death have only been

130

spoken of since it became necessary to establish the fact of her death <u>in connection with this claim</u> for pension."

So here, we depart the truth, whatever it is. Jacob Bowles spent seemingly endless years pursuing a pension that was always beyond his reach. Eventually, he got a little bit, which was subsequently expanded by Congressional decree. Able to enjoy the benefits for a season, the inevitable crept in, and he soon died. His widow must now pursue the same pension, hopefully able to navigate the bureaucracy which she faced. All the strange implications which are raised during this process are never really cleared to anyone's satisfaction.

It would be far more difficult to produce a fictional account.

www.ingramcontent.com/pod-product-compliance
Lightning Source LLC
Chambersburg PA
CBHW051321170526
45166CB00002B/641